WRITE UNTIL YOU CRY

A JIMMY SANTIAGO BACA WORKSHOP ANTHOLOGY

WRITE UNTIL YOU CRY

FLOWERSONG
PRESS

A JIMMY SANTIAGO BACA
WORKSHOP ANTHOLOGY

FLOWERSONG
PRESS

FlowerSong Press
Copyright © 2024 by FlowerSong Press and individual authors
ISBN: 978-1-963245-61-5

Published by FlowerSong Press
in the United States of America.
www.flowersongpress.com

Edited by Veronica C. Evans
Cover Art by Lonnie Anderson

Production Editor: Avery C. Castillo
Acquiring/Commissioning Editor: Natalie Sierra
Cover Design: Edward Vidaurre
Typesetting: Priscilla Celina Suarez
Set in Adobe Garamond Pro

NOTICE: SCHOOLS AND BUSINESSES
FlowerSong Press offers copies of this book at quantity discount with bulk purchase
for educational, business, or sales promotional use. For information, please email the
Publisher at info@flowersongpress.com.

CONTENTS

Introduction

In June of 2023, fresh and unleashed from America's covid crisis, a room full of excited poets gathered for the Annual Jimmy Santiago Baca Writers Retreat, held at the Albuquerque Museum. Besides the expected daily workshops, we were surprised to receive sessions on ecstatic dancing, hip-hop verses, gardening, native ceremonial movements, and an opportunity to learn a Buddhist chant. In his words, we were invited to 'loosen up the subconscious enough to allow the ego to step aside for the writer/poet to write'. And loosen up we did!

Toward the end of that retreat, he announced it as his tenth and, most likely, final workshop. Looks of surprise were evident on every face. I heard murmurs of respectful push back from everyone. Who wants to lose a poet of this stature, a person who has worked so diligently to unearth his own excellence up from the depths of a wounded heart/ life and be able to do the same for so many other writers, often stuck in their own fields of daily challenge? Our respect and appreciation for his body of work, spanning more than 40 years, exploded in applause while a personal vow that this retreat would not be his last quietly arose in my heart.

We came together after this momentous event and decided to honor our mentor with a book of original poetry. We wanted those unfamiliar with his life's work to awaken to his unique ability to unearth the talent lying beneath the surface of so many different kinds of people, from so many different cultures in the span of a few days.

His ability to develop and encourage everyone, to take them from where they stand and to confidently rise to their unique greatness proved his mastery in understanding and valuing the person standing right in front of him. We felt more artists needed the opportunity to be so richly impacted.

This book is the culmination of each writer's heart, heritage, and culture, their past and promise of a dynamic future, and their unique joys and sorrows. As you look at the bios of these writers, you will see abundant, rich and diverse talent. What you won't be privy to are the immense obstacles, sudden barriers and monumental pressures many faced during that brilliant summer of camaraderie and newfound freedom.

We invite you to join us at future retreats and experience your own development and growth as you put pen to paper and express what humanity looks like from your own perspective.

—Veronica Evans
Editor

WRITE UNTIL YOU CRY

I Know You Know

ADAMS, VICTORIA

I knew you at 14
When I seemed so much older,
Distanced from those around me.

I knew you at 19
When I fled in a blizzard
Scared, hurt, aching for answers.

I knew you at 21
When I walked out
No longer fearing a letter of red.

I knew you at 28
When you threatened
My life if I left.

Oh, yes, I knew you
Whatever face you wore.
And I learned that face, that voice.

Now it matters not
Whose face you use,
Or how that voice can make me shudder.

I know you now
And you've lost the key
To cause me fear or pain.

Now you must know this:
My fury lives, deep within the weariness.
And silence is not an option.

It Is Time - Past Time

ADAMS, VICTORIA

I can't feel your pain.
I've tried, I even thought I knew
How you felt.
Scared
Alone
With nowhere to go,
No safe place to know,
It would all be fine.
I can't feel your pain.
I've tried, by reaching back
All those years,
When I was abused,
Bullied,
Stalked,
Manipulated,
Frightened, and alone.

I can't feel your pain.
I've been tired,
I've been hungry,
Depressed,
Trapped.
Even, yes, even
Had my life threatened.
But I always found a way,
A way to live another day.

Perhaps I understand,
In some small way,
How deep the ache,

How sore
Your soul.
But now I see,
It never goes away.
For you it's every day.

The air you breathe,
The ground you walk,
Is filled with hate,
And fear,
And terror.
Barely in the shadows,
But growing ever stronger,
Reaching for us all.

As hard as I try,
It seems no more
Than insult,
to your
Torn,
and battered
Heart,
to say,
I feel your pain.

Perhaps, as small
As it may be,
My voice can help,
My life can show,
That hate
is never,
ever,
ever,
the answer.
For the love of all
Creation has provided,
It is time.

It is time to end the pain.
It is time to be there
For the black,
For the Muslim,
For the gay,
For the PEOPLE,
Of our earth.
One person at a time.

I will do my best.
I will share.
I will talk.
I will try to reach
Minds,
And hearts.
And I will hope.
I will not say,
I feel your pain.
But I will be here.
I will hold you.
And one day, together,
We will find the dawn.

To Be a Giver of Flight

ADAMS, VICTORIA

To see the spark

You ignite

Fuel the puff that lifts the wing

To loose the cords

That bind the imagination

And watch the creature

Thus inspired

Grow before your very eyes.

A taste of pride

That must have been

Endured by gods of old

And yet a deep humility

To understand

What small and timely

Gifts of self

A word, a thought,

A helping hand

Can spur a destiny

Found Library

AGUILAR, DAHLIA

My father comes home
books in tow
what he cannot afford. Gathered from service lanes
and dumpster shadows. I
stacked them proudly
in my closet library.

Alleyway encyclopedia
The Ocean World of Jacques Cousteau
slight mildew on rear cover
Color photos! Mammoth whales and oceans blue!

Edgar Allan Poe, from papi's
high school days at Jefferson.
Read us The Raven every Halloween.

Hospital Corps United States Navy Handbook.
Study scientific drawings. Believed
I could use Goody hair ribbons to treat a fractured patella.

Hans Christian Andersen the darkest volume
where I read and reread the Little Match Girl
hoping for a different end before sleep.

Frankie

AGUILAR, DAHLIA

Frankie plays piano far left of sanctuary.
Fifteen hardwood oak pews separate us.
Mama doesn't like to sit far back or front at church.
Summer light radiates through windows of Sacred Heart,
Spotlights my cousin, glares his glasses,
Illuminates his graceful brown hands.

People file into church. A minor key surrenders
to the theme song from *Terms of Endearment*.
I stop forbidden laughter. Cupped hand to mouth.
His eyes catch mine. I send thumbs up.
"What?" Mama asks. I nod no. Nothing.
The priest lights the candles at the altar.

I whisper to mama, *"Do you know Frankie taught himself to play piano?
All on his own! How to read music, too? Never took a lesson!"*
Heels click along the marble floor as the last parishioners
take their hymnals and bench seats.
Mama taps me on the shoulder. Signals genuflection.

Sweaty knees steady on vinyl cushioned kneeler.
Mass begins. Frankie transitions to *Make Me a Channel of Your Peace*.
When I was little I wondered if it was a TV channel
As I grew older, if it was a boat channel.
Papi says neither. Only a metaphor.
Mama rolls an iridescent crucifix
crystal between her fingers.

Where there is darkness only light.
Incense escape ornate openings of the swinging brass thurible.
People turn over their shoulders to snicker. The last person
Struggles to open heavy wooden doors.
Rushes through a watery sign of the cross.
Arrives after mass has been called to order.

Oh, Master grant that I may never seek.
So much to be consoled as to console.
I ask Mama, *"Why shouldn't we ask?*
as much to be consoled? Isn't that prayer?"
Shh! She mimes.

Frankie knows, I decide. He consoles more
than he asks to be consoled.
To be understood as to understand
To be loved as to love with all my soul.
My primo plays church piano, making it
Beautiful even for the non believers.
My fingers find themselves tip to tip.
Frankie moves on to the theme song
from *Fried Green Tomatoes.*

I giggle this time out loud.
Another movie theme song.
This one from a film about
Racism and southern lesbian heroines.
I love you, Frankie.
Reverence whispered like a prayer.

Spit Quick

AGUILAR, DAHLIA

The man that raised you wears
suspenders and dickies with no undershirt.
Perches on the adobe steps that cannot divide
your home from summer.

When Burque heat turns the children
against one another, he slaps his hands together
making dust of restlessness.

He raises a hand,
shouts, *You can go to the store, but*
you better be back before that spit dries.

He spits on the ground,
the challenge claps your heart
race start pistol.

The sprint underway
Olympic speed for glory,
you buy him cigarettes, yourselves jawbreakers.

You run cross the finish line
back to the steps,
giggling with glee when he declares,
Just in time, just in time!

A Love Letter to My Body

BERRY, SHAVAWN M.

"What would happen if one woman told the truth about her life? The world would split open."

—Muriel Rukeyser

My body. The perimeter of me. The country I inhabit. Lined by borders and ancient trees. I am a rag mopping up the world's mess. A slippery container for my soul-story, the skin of my skin, the breath of my breath. I'm an empath, and a highly sensitive intuitive. An introvert and a tuning fork for all bullshit and bravado that crosses my path.

My brain crackles inside my skull, neurodivergent, elastic, imaginative, other-worldly. I give thanks for this body.

I give props to its bumpy skin, broken blood vessels, and in-grown nails.

I love the marrow of this metaphorical cashmere coat, the one that wraps me in a fortress of flesh, all soft curves, no jutting bones.

I am grateful for all the ways in which I have learned to move through the world in this body – this body of a diabetic with sleep apnea, high blood pressure, high cholesterol, and depression. But I am not only what ails me.

I am thankful and blessed to live in this body. This gift. This moment-to-moment container of sweet honey and worker bees, lavender spinning toward my center.

When I was first diagnosed with diabetes, I looked up Louise Hay's definition of it in *You Can Heal Your Life*. She said I had *too little sweetness* then, and she was right. She sent an arrow of clarity straight through my chest.

At the time, I worked a Sisyphean job – 60 hours a week – bereft and joyless. I needed a change.

That lack of sweetness – that lack of insulin – that legacy my father left me with his unruly brows and hooded eyes, with his identical short upper lip, and the tendency to sing myself to sleep – that ended up saving *this body*, this soul, this woman on the verge. It saved me from my tendency to use food as comfort rather than nourishment. It showed me what it meant to practice self-care.

> *"True self-care is not salt baths and chocolate cake, it is making the choice to build a life you don't need to regularly escape from."*

> —Brianna Weist

I feel blessed by my scars – the one crossing under my bottom lip – the one I got when face-planting the day after Thanksgiving in 2013 while walking to the store to buy cherry pie filling. The scar on my right knee, the result of my flying off the stairs of a double-decker bus in London, hitting the sidewalk in a great rush of tangled feet and clothing, blood staining my skirt, ripping my pale pink tights. The resulting coin-shaped scar led to me enjoying a cup of tea in a flat with two strangers. They dressed my wound, gave me a chocolate biscuit, and sent me on my way.

I can trace my scars from chicken pox, measles, and all the places where my cats have swiped me, drawing blood, scabbing over.

I remember my broken left and right wrist, my surgeries – the scraping of my uterus, the removal of cysts and fibroids – as well as the plastic surgeon who repaired my bottom lip when I put my teeth through it.

I am thankful my tonsils and adenoids float in a jar of alcohol somewhere – or do they - cut out when I was just four.

I am grateful for all of it: the tenderness, the aches, the loss of my perfect 20/20 vision, the silver hair growing in when I moved to New Mexico.

I remember all the versions of this body I've inhabited: the tiny embryonic, clump of cells in my mother's womb, the thumb-sucking, squalling baby, once born; the toddler going for a walk when my father was meant to be watching me.

My frantic mother found me an hour later, in a soaked diaper, watching a softball game at the school where I would end up going to kindergarten. I had walked more than a mile from home, crossing several busy intersections.

I recall the seven- and eight-year-old girl pedaling her bicycle through fields of sweet onions, without fear. With absolutely no fear.

I still harbor the teen, long fringe of hair in her eyes, whose period started at 12 and lasted until 53.

I love the kindness I feel toward my body. It houses my soul.

At 63, I revel in the rumpled bed I've become, slept in, stacked with pillows, surrounded by books, reading glasses, and lemon water.

Reading Room

BERRY, SHAVAWN M.

As you sleep, lenticular clouds cross overhead.
They lie on their backs blocking the Sangre de Cristos.

Your face contains a hundred different kinds
Of clouds – soaring cumulus, sun-silvered mackerel,

a smear of slow-moving cirrus, nimbostratus swollen with rain.
Your palette's filled with blues:

robin's egg, flax, blue bonnet, violent thunderhead,
A barn owl dive-bombing its prey.

You breathe in indigo; you breathe out violet-blue
air stinging with the scent of lilacs in summer.

You dream of hawks. A bonded pair stretches and floats
On a small river of wind, bee pollen dusting their wings.

Clouds speckle your face as I watch you.
Each cloud a syllable, a line, a story, a word.

I long to read the cloudy tea leaves trailing after
You as you emerge from sleep, groggy, hair a mess.

I long to read the Braille of your skin and know you.

Reading Room, included in the collection, Evanescent Creature: Poems & Meditations,
to be published by Golden Dragonfly Press, March 28, 2023

When The Weariness of Your Day

BERRY, SHAVAWN M.

feels like too much --
too much noise,
too much chatter,
too much, unsettled darkness.
Remember
Even oak trees rest, even the dry grasses
beneath your feet sleep
even the snow falling, feather-light,
each flake completely different from the last,
slows down, swirls in the clear air,
& Comes to rest on your eyelashes
If you need to breathe, breathe
If you need to sleep, sleep
If you need to pause, pause
Focus on the smallest sliver of time
Focus on the whorls
Stamped concentrically on your fingertips
Focus on that white scar on your left knee
The world will wait for you to catch up.

When The Weariness of Your Day, included in the collection, Evanescent Creature: Poems & Meditations, to be published by Golden Dragonfly Press, March 28, 2023

Dream of Tata

CARDONA, LUPE CARRASCO

Oh, Tata, grace me in the realm of dreams tonight,
Entrance me as once we yearned, too timid to embark -
Like a kite bereft of a master's gentle hand, set adrift,
To wander aimlessly, severed from its cherished home.

Transport me far, where your eyes beheld with love,
So deeply cherished, it tore you from our earthly realm,
While we struggled to learn, to love, to merely exist,
Let us ascend together, witness both beauty and despair.

To read once more by your side, dear Tata,
Of Sitting Bull's unyielding tenacity, relentless and bold,
Of Che Guevara's fervent love, carved from his very soul,
And the enchantment of Ultima's mystical domain.

Sing to me, Tata, let your voice echo with tenderness,
Call me "mijita," a cherished endearment on your lips,
Weave my *trenzas* with colorful yarn, tenderly braid,
Tell me, with wisdom born of years, bathing remains optional.

May your contagious passion ignite within my core,
For our people, our heritage, our exquisite essence,
Despite the illusion, we are anything but ordinary,
Guided by your teachings, I yearn to become a healer.

Oh, Tata, embrace me in dreams, so ethereal and grand,
Grant me the strength to walk in the footsteps of magic,
To heal, to nurture, for within me lies the power,
And you, my beloved Tata, are the source of inspiration.

My *Abuelita's* Liberation
CARDONA, LUPE CARRASCO

I find myself entwined in a federal lawsuit's cruel grasp for speaking ancestral stories in the sacred classroom. I'm being sued for counter-storytelling and for fighting for all Native People and People of Color to have the right to counter-storytell too. Case No. 2:22-cv-03243-FMO

As a CHICANA teacher, I endure toxic disdain, *Anything But Mexican*, a shared tale not just confined to Rudy Acuña's literary and historical domain. Gringos continuously hurl "mongrel" and "half-breed", in their vicious spite. Too indigenous and of color to be white (no desire to be anyway) and too mongrel to be indigenous. Imagine existing as a blue-eyed Chicana, adorned with the dichotomy of grace and derision, embodying the duality of both invasive conqueror and healer like your ancestral curandera, *mi abuelita Guadalupe*. I embody pain's touch and mending grace, a paradox of darkness and solace brought on by conquistadors' rape.

So I'm being sued by well-resourced Zionists with a lot of time on their hands. Of all the thousands of activists, scholars, and organizers in the struggle for Chicanx and Ethnic Studies, three women of color are being sued. CECILY MYART-CRUZ, AFRO-CHICANA UTLA president THERESA MONTANO, Chicana Profesora AND me, GUADALUPE CARRASCO CARDONA, five foot tall shape shifting *Chicana* who won't back down to no one because my tata taught me well. My childhood lessons included Zapata's cry of land and liberty, Petra Herrera's brigada feminina, and from the river to the sea, Palestina will be free. No one should live without the dignity of acknowledging their roots, tears and blood in their land.

§

During my time in 7th grade, I would stroll back home alongside Evan, a young Euro-American fellow who resided in a community of upper-middle class abodes halfway to my apartment complex. On a particular day as we reached our parting spot north of the train tracks, where he would turn left and I would continue on my way to the other side of town, he kindly informed me of a joke he wished to share, emphasizing the importance of not taking offense. My heart dropped but my curiosity piqued, Well what is it? "Mexicans are proof that Indians fucked buffalos."

What the fuck? I didn't have the language to understand or to be able to respond to what had just happened. All I knew was that in my mind I was like, "fuck that kid!" and I stopped walking with him from school.

Luckily, before that happened to me, my tata, my Father, Antonio Isidoro Medrano Carrasco, an anti-imperialist, Chicano hippy, an artivist before that was even a word, and a barrio intellectual of *el movimiento* used to say to me, "mija, you're not going to be a sellout. You're Mexicana, you're a Chicana, be proud of your ancestors and make them proud of you!"

I held that deep in my soul to protect me from all the master narratives of being a mongrel and my *abuelitas* fucking buffalos.

I had nothing but my tata to free me from the shame of being *una hija de la chingada.* I had no Chicanx Studies, no Ethnic Studies, just the core curriculum in kindergarten to high school, just mainstream tv and Hollywood. All of that education, in and out of the classroom, taught us to revere those who look like and think like Evan.

§

My abuelita Guadalupe understood the Earth medicine and how to pray to the Creator for healing. When she was born in *Julimes, Chihuahua, Mexico,* she had to bury her spirituality deep in the cloth of the Catholic Church. Her Apache *raices* grounded her despite centuries of uprooting that took form in all spaces and places of education. She knew and understood that she was an indigenous woman and she also understood that the only way that she could express it was to silently embed it in her sacred Catholic Church. It wasn't until she knew she was near the end that she spoke proudly about her Apache heritage.

"Mija, I would talk to your *abuelita* about her *abuelitas* and how it used to be in the olden days. It made her very happy to share these stories with me. She firmly rooted me until one morning in 1973 when I woke up early. I could feel that something was not right. I walked to the front of the house where she slept."

My tata found her where she took her last breath, on her back, with her wrists and ankles tied with red yarn, her palms facing up with coins resting inside them. She wanted to become an ancestor the way her *abuelitas* taught her, like an Apache.

She was only 54 years old, a mother of 12 and grandmother of many. Her untimely demise was not a result of an incurable heart condition, but rather a heartbreaking consequence of the unwarranted shame she felt when seeking medical help. As an indigenous Mexican woman with numerous children and limited English proficiency, she was unjustly subjected to judgments and prejudice from those entrusted with her care. So she avoided institutional medicine like the plague.

§

My tata taught me to, "... be proud of who you are and where you come from," but institutions treated his mother, my mother, me, all the *mujeres* of my life, like the spawn of the buffalo. We all responded differently to this oppression.

My *tias* dropped out and got married at the age of 16. My *primas* were pushed out of school, escaped home at all costs, babies at 14, 16, 17. Internalized oppression, self-hatred for being Mexican, a woman, dark, a victim of abuse.

How did I respond? Not much differently. I resisted school, AP in Euro-American bullshit was like watching paint dry and I wanted to be inspired and feel alive. I ditched regularly throughout high school. I wanted to "find" myself but all I found was friendship with other traumatized *Chicanitas* who did not have a tata reminding them that they should... "be proud of your ancestors and make them proud of you!" More trauma, graduation from Frontier Continuation High School, mother at 18.

My mom never told me to go to college. For her, success was measured in not getting pregnant when you're still in high school and not collecting welfare. In the year 1995, much to my mom's initial dismay, I embarked on an incredible journey of motherhood and simultaneously enrolled in a thought-provoking Chicanx Studies class at Oxnard

Community College.I was like holy shit. I can earn a college degree, learn from counter-storytellers of color about the ancestors, and make my tata proud at the same time. That was the beginning of my journey as a ferocious learner and lover of books; Always Running, Bless Me, Ultima, A Place to Stand. Wtf, stories that spoke to me and disrupted the master narrative nudged me free.

I love you Chicanx Studies. I will continue to fight for you Ethnic Studies. They picked the wrong badass, hella fucking proud, *chingona*, don't give a fuck, will take my earrings off If I have to Chicana *maestra* to fuck with. Take your lawsuit and wipe your ass with it. Ethnic Studies isn't about you, this isn't your story EVAN and your racist dehumanizing joke about my people and the buffalo. Ethnic Studies is about loving ourselves and loving our beautiful, short, and hella strong *abuelitas* who suffered, and endured, but lived long enough for us to be here today.

This is how I came to *know* myself, and to be worth anything for myself and for anyone else, through Chicanx Studies at Oxnard Community College in the 90's. In the depths of my Chicana existence, I once found myself ensnared within an inescapable abyss of self-doubt and hopelessness. Now I strive to emancipate my Chicana soul and embrace a sense of completeness in this world filled with self-loathing and horizontal violence which I now reject and combat. Now I am liberated and with an open hand, I invite each and every one of you to join me on this incredible journey. The fight for Ethnic Studies transcends time, not only embracing the next seven generations but also paying homage to the seven generations that came before us.

Long live Guadalupe Medrano Carrasco… long live Abelia Aguirre Padilla… long live all the *abuelitas*, all the ancestors, and long live Chicanx and Ethnic Studies.

Ixukeni

CARDONA, RAÚL

Where did it go?
Can't say I know,
Those times of evolution.

Pobre de ti,

Nothing but chaos and confusion.
Tale unfolds at our home gates.
Birth zone of history grates.
Forefathers who couldn't wait,
To steal, murder and regulate.
Formulate.

Repossessed our soils.
What you call United States?
Land of the free, while sitting on Tribal estates.
Offering to pay absurd rates

Grandfather time and mother earth wanted us to innovate,
This land greed's decided to confiscate.
Swiping swords, you annihilated.
Blasting guns, you assassinated.

We've got to question why you've got this hate.
Forefathers could not wait.
So, they took the devils bate.
Felt this need to demonstrate,
The power to eliminate.

What goes around comes around let's set that level straight.
Every pig has his day, the righteous too will celebrate.

Born tangled in this web before we give our lives a chance.
No time to enhance, no time to romance,
With the idea of making dreams come true for me and you.
From the school of hard knocks to the penitentiary we graduate
Our four sides gated,
On the inside we're educated.
Better late than never.
Whatever. However.
Forever, deal with that pain.
Takes a life time to explain.
Aqui te vengo,
Walking and talking through verses on the horizon.
Who laid their railroads over our pathways obstructing harmonics?
Who gave you precious metals in exchange you gave us bubonic?
Musical soundscapes in time reflect us plagued by the ironic
Cry of the surrealist Olmeca, Purhepecha chronicles.
Michoacan poetry through simple mathematics,
Transplanted Zavuya Skywatchers early Chilam pragmatics.
Jaguar que corres por Califas breathing semi-psychotic.
Who's got the rhythm and tempo to keep you moving aquatic?

Well If you know your mathematics,
Then you know I'm the one.
Speaking in this foreign tongue
With my people of the sun.

If you want to breathe again track this,
Looking all contrived with the methods that you've practiced.
Why you sweating my friend? Can't you hack this?
I got a piece of advice for you, practice!

A new approach to the way that you've done it.
Change it up, slow it down, maybe learn it.

Catch your balance right quick before you burn it.
Then perhaps righteously your will earn it.

And you will know if your way wasn't working
Cause all this time that you spent was it jerking?
And in the final analysis you will see,
You should've loved yourself more instead of hating on me.

But don't you take it from me just take a look within,
Whatever slowing you down don't let it happen again.
You got to know life is precious every second counts.
So, one more thing my relatives right before I bounce.

May beauty be above us. May beauty be below us.
May beauty be all around us. Peace.

Kids from Gas Station Hell

COUPERUS, VANCE

There's a lonely Speedway gas station in Romeroville, just outside of Las Vegas, New Mexico. Loose soil blusters into projectiles. Eastwood eyes squint. Blowing trash roots in awkward berms along the acreage-large barbed-wire fencing. Sounds of something clanging out yonder. They ventilated Todder out front. Shattered storefront monsoons of glass and red spray aerosol. Cauliflower clouds unmoored overhead.

That old corduroy jacket with fake sheep wool lining? His signature? Ruined. Shot trough. Todder died with an erection, they say. He used to prune cottonwoods, was fond of a meandering guitar.

Inside, the old filling station pulls at soles en route to the bathroom. Smells like rancid butter. There are ersatz petroglyph tiles centered above the urinals, factory made: elk, bears, warrior horseriders, and beavers suspended in manically clever concavities.

Due to an outskirt deportment, this station is held up less than other places.

Giddy though, a metabolic lowlier with COPD, the petrol terminal has trouble exhaling. Lungs of unspittable ponderosa needles.

Travelers who do stop are rendered giants by their vehicles, even when they are diminished. Locals behind the registers were born poor, raised brown, and watch people and autos stare through the nametags. Everyday – glint, glean, grit and sunblind, dry-socket, jagged tooth. Once in a while, a local hooligan will drive the few miles south along I-25 to test out the sensual healing of violence, discover how much is in the drawers and khaki pockets, how much blood is in the cranium or what is embayed behind the tints.

Dick, slit, tits, and twine. Cigarettes. Love. Social currency. Desperation fondled.

Nouns larger than conception and stature. Immersive subjectives. Oceans. Primrose.

Zeke was found in woman's lingerie in Lincoln Park, drunk after running out of money and bathtub crank rock, the predawn sky a memory-match for his pallor.

Biblical Ezekiel had devastated his nipples with lit cigarettes, his chapped smile too much as they bent his head into the police cab. An acute experiencer, his efforts bespoken, his bare feet bloodied.

Most are arrested, tie-down roped, heel-drug, hung. They play tag with hatchets.

On the high prairie the wind shoots clean currents and avian skeletons. 6,435 feet rarified. The grass is folded downward in napkins. Skirling shadows of birds.

Marriage Toast to Two Children Without Parents (S+N)

COUPERUS, VANCE

There isn't enough blood in the world, but there are aphids with a collectively beautiful gait. Have you seen them? They bleed sugar, white like sexual discharge. I want a gamboling dog in Melody Park to be enough; the red and off-ivory checkers of a picnic blanket becoming the conquerable sky through which ants erupt from to be enough;

the idea of the family of self and the family of others to be enough; I want the swollen purple Maine blueberries for Sal, the mordant tongue-ink and safe-stewarding bear to be enough; my arm in the grass around love, one hand tangling in the froths of baby Eddy's ebony hair, the other hand in mere creation

with her book, her words, her vodka wringing out the most beautiful water I have inside me. I ruin it. I cry. Baby Eddy's dead in New Mexico. Or at least he's not a baby anymore. Either way, he doesn't cry. I want this to be enough. Still, I pick about and try to pry stars out of a Roman puddle. I have dusty hands.

Rough hands. Hands I've used to trod wine vermillion. I slip a finger inside her. The realization that this is the most important effort afforded feels enough. A conflation between violence & kindness is real. They exchange rings, they play Knock-Knock at Paddy Freeman's under the Chiming Tree. Violent kindness has come to me at times

and shared me raw. Be still. I want to feel your cheek on my ribbed cage and understand that you are breathing only from the brittle itch of your sweat. The sole need is to feel present with you and alone with myself. Will I be enough? Semen and ambulance? Will capitalized letters from a stranger be enough?

Santa Rosa

COUPERUS, VANCE

Walled in on 3 sides by cinderblocks and slats, our backyard garden is a clock of sunlight, dervish skinks, and mendicant mice. We learn about paper wasps, the parasitic eggs they lay inside of horned caterpillars. The larva eat their way through. I thought that it was only tarantula wasps that did this. Displace size, I mean. I saw one once in real life. Not in our garden, but in Santa Rosa, the Hidden Lake, right where the water knocked at the sandstone.

A wasp the size of my open hand was aloft and dragging the body of an ebony tarantula up the slope, away from someone's smatter of feces and discarded TP. The black of the arachnid was dense. Midnight formation and needle hair of that creature pulled and ate everything that wasn't white and blinding, vibrated in inertia. We understood, as the wasp struggled with the spider, that the tarantula was paralyzed, that eggs were already ripping nourishment from the body of the aware. Do insects feel pain, we wondered? Do stars? Do holes? There's the Blue Hole not too far away, where the tourists go. There is no guilt without disorder. But there is disorder without guilt, a pregnancy of death.

That night, drunk on Tecate and other things, illegally camping, we climbed the cliff. Just two of us. Thinking ourselves brave. I was the one with the theory that the stars and night sky were reflected on the water of Hidden Lake, and that if we jumped that 40 feet downwards, it would be like jumping into the Stellar, into the Endless, into Space. It was. Both of us lost track of the surface, couldn't find the proprioception to brace ourselves, and with no focal point to fall to, to resist against, we were unbalanced, landing sideways in the water, almost colliding. My right arm felt like it had been ripped from its socket and put back as I tried to swim out. Yours was different, but the same. For weeks. Rip is a circumpolar term, a compass machine stitching the red flutterings inside to the outsides, memories according to necessity.

Where do we go now? In the garden the chard is burnt and I suspect it is because of the soil. We dug down. It was like concrete. There were galvanized nails and stucco, and commercial insulation and shit like that. It had settled. We composted, turned the feces of animals into it, bespoke our efforts, made love and penetrated all night in the dirt. In our backyard, years have passed, and there are now ensnarled tomatoes growing that stretch so far that they break stake, stalk, and structure, and there are hornworms in abundance eating the voluptuous plant bodies. The paper wasps come, buzz, and lay parasitic eggs on the green worms. I kneel and leap into the shade of the tomatoes. There are purple, bursting tomatoes. Heirlooms, of a sort. I hope that you are late. Or maybe that you don't come home. Again. Are we but what we recall? I itch behind my ear but I can't locate the polysyllables of your name. It comes as a quiet rush.

Poem

CRAWFORD, MERIAH L.

Begin with a shout-out to a god or lover or fancy bird;
Continue with a heartfelt plea to the moon that you be heard.
Add in a lavish description of a field or brook or wood,
Preparing a nested metaphor that will rarely be understood.

A reference to a long-dead friend would not be amiss,
Or tales of your brave victory over some grave illness.
Bare your aching heart over the loss of one who made you whole;
Share the suffering of your once-unconquerable soul.

Gaze rapt at the stars glinting like diamonds in the heavens,
At irises, orchids, lilies, and roses by the dozens.
Cry out to the shining ship that passes in the night,
And sigh, sigh, for the perfect poem that fades with dawn's first light.

Summer at The Beach

CRAWFORD, MERIAH L.

Waves curling and drawing,
forward, back,
cycling, recycling,
tossing treasures on the sand.
Shells, bones, seaweed, trash.
Pretty shells and Slim Jim wrappers,
Coke cans and dead crabs.
And the salt tang,
and the stiff breeze,
and the crunch and slide of the sand underfoot.
Every so often a seal or a sailboat passes by.
Every so often a fish or a dolphin washes up dead.
On a good day, the beach is yours.
On a bad day? Sunburn and loud music and screaming kids.
Ups. Downs.
Ice cream cones and a cold beer.
Bad clams and rip tides.
And always the certainty of more.
Always next year.

Cleaner, dirtier.
Cooler, warmer.
Sharks, maybe.
Pelicans, perhaps.
Jellyfish, always.
Shifting dunes,
and different décor.
A hermit crab in a round mesh cage.
A small white box of fudge.
T-shirts: 50% off.

But stand on the sand
and look outwards.
Look away from now
into forever.
Take one deep breath.
Another.
Another.
Feel the water draw the sand

from under your feet.
Sink into the cool water,
and let it flow,
ebb,
flow.

Eulogy for An Estranged Mother
DELEEUW, JOSHUA

breathing, techno, courage
where do I stand
overrun by loss, my mother, gone forever
i sit here, cobal in the air, sacred scent of the ancestors
golden spiral, Om, Rage

bitterness like crushed Ritalin and little dixie cups of water
gritty thoughts transcend even the breath of things
writing again in lined pages in search of clarity

oh mother, can you hear me now
out there in the wind, amongst the trees, amongst the rocks
i careen through time as the wheels of my motorcycle
hit the yellow dotted lines of the freeway
returning to a place i have never known comfort
a mother's home that is not a refuge
it is a curse of yesterdays tears
binding my heart in shackles of regret
i am so sorry, wishing we had more time
in a life filled with time, my heart is beating

i shall return to your womb as I blaze through
the slot canyons of Apache country
i travel like the absence of drums in a beat
into the womb of the Great Mother, the center of things
back to her in the earth, back to her in the road
returning back to the absence, the lack of you,
in my daily routine
no longer concerned with how my words shall cut you,
rip away the dark veil you put over your face to escape

flashbacks and rape, leaving sons and daughters
crawling out of the darkness and leaving us behind

i am a nowhere boy, drifting along without destination
returning to a home that has never been a safe haven
when never becomes forever, tears pierce my eyes
there is no more time, no more patience, no more tomorrow
there is only now, without you
your breath gone, your body turned to ash

i am left with a lack of memories
its been 14 years since i looked into your eyes
since i touched your skin and smelled your hair
since i saw myself in your long stare as we reflected
on all the stories we never had

together, never, always at a distance, always from afar
i have longed to care for you
to bring you water and breakfast, to light your cigarette
and give you lectures on your health
to drive you to the grocery store
to help you slice vegetables for your lasagna

if you ever called i would have dropped my world
changed my stars, put a thumb out
I would have ran to you
the phone never rang, the letter never came
only sadness and rage and regret

the last time i heard your voice you were kind
you were proud of me
as a father, as a servant, as a healer
i will keep those words close to my heart

i remember you, warrior woman
mother on the run
i will always love the idea of you

Homeless

ELLIOTT, SHARON

woman with kids

on the edge
you have to know
how not to be poor
and they don't teach that in school

frozen bone
inaccessible marrow
endless
unfulfillable expectations
reflections in department store windows

living on the streets
Nintendo is
an expletive
shaming kids
who ain't got one

free food is under nourishing
making a roly poly statement
of fat and flesh
it's hard to receive benefits
or apply for a job
without an address
and then
rent isn't covered
bills
clothes
school supplies
let alone food

day is a waking burden
long hot cement
beneath aching feet
struggles to find a doorway
an alley
to take a piss
later
searching for one
that doesn't smell like piss
to rest in
sleepy time a nightmare

washing hungry little faces
in gas station bathrooms
that no longer exist
key or no key
raggedy clothes
smelling
like years of no detergent

the hum and roll
of a dryer in a warm laundry room
dreams fading into mist
cold apple juice from a fridge
grilled-cheese sandwich
are legends
bare feet
in green grass
not a choice anymore
but a requiem

Gutters & Alleyways – Perspectives on Poverty and Struggle, pg. 60, October 2014,
Lucid Moose Lit, pub., Nancy Lynée Wood & Sarah Thursday, eds.

Violent Domesticity

ELLIOTT, SHARON

what is it
they want
when they break a woman

wring her eyes dry
into a room
no bigger than a shot glass

carve her bones
into
a leftover casserole

sift her blood
into a bend
in the river

gag her
with her
own tongue

it must be
nothing
a momentary leap of groin

a game of tag
with eternity
theirs not hers
or maybe
the only something they can feel
is her suffering

through their
hands
her heart is broken

pumps only
at their whim
from its place underfoot

a power
so intoxicating
they refuse her escape

keep her breath
in a box
by the fireplace

like a match
to burnish
the night

Il Golem Femmina, 8/16/2015, translation into Italian by Met Sambiase,
https://metsambiase.wordpress.com/2015/08/16/violent-domesticity-sharon-elliot-
riapre-la-poesia-del-golemfemmina/

La Bloga on-line Floricanto, 6/2/2015,
http://labloga.blogspot.com/2015/06/la-palabra-wraps-may-muralists-of-la-on.html

At The Ritz

HUTCHINSON, SUSAN A.

He sat in the tub

waxing on about Hemingway

with his iced vodka, a deep pour

And in that baptismal water

I washed his troubled head

The lather cleansing his sorrows

if only for that brief soak

in Canadian water.

He asked me in

But I declined

Wise to the ways of his

Insobriety and inner shame.

But if I had said, "Yes, I will join you"

The water that we shared

would have leapt high like a fountain in Venice

And spiraled down and around us

in waves of oceanic embrace.

Burn

HUTCHINSON, SUSAN A.

That scar above your knee

Was it the Summer on Nantucket when you were 18

And those white cord bracelets, woven in a way that eclipsed the braid

Burned at the cut ends as clasp, closure

All the rage, as they say

You succumbed, new bearer of the novelty

An adolescent initiation.

For future memoir, perhaps

What was to become testifiable.

As you fit the complex weaving on your wrist, lit the match

Liquifying the cording

A fiery ball of melted nylon fell

Penetrating your lower thigh, a drop of molten lava

The burn penetrating layer after layer

Flesh cratering ferociously, furiously

The flame of treason, unreason its mistress

And the Mexican peasant dress, a chambray cotton of the finest construction

Hung helplessly, the hem inches away from the assault

And a shriek that only Lucifer could hear

Commemorated the occasion.

The Granite Fish

HUTCHINSON, SUSAN A.

As she drew near to the splash of the koi fountain, her Japanese statuary that had sat readied for decades in tousled lawn weeds, a run of stifled, salty tears freed themselves from a reservoir of loss and betrayal. The watery sorrow, born from years of dreams decimated by naivete and disloyalty, always turned her eyes from hazel to a luminescent, Mediterranean green. And being born under the sign of the fish, and in the presence of the granite fish fountain, her emotions would liquify into a soothing melt.

Overlooked and abandoned, she felt an irrepressible communion with this fixture, now incarnated in its purposed destiny as a vessel for the irresistible singsong of flowing water and silken splash.

River stones from the oceanic shores of Mexico had been delivered to the house in 50 pound bags, and she arranged them with great care and purpose around the base where the tailfin swept up in a show of aquatic, flippant pose. The carver must have been a craftsman of profound and masterful skill, she mused, because the scales and proportions were as perfect as the Golden Mean. And in that carving she was to find her solace and ultimately discover her own impassioned purpose.

Each day she went to the fountain and sat in her writing chair, feet perched on the cedar footrest, the white, cast metal side table accommodating her Rubinato ink and Raika notepad. In this seat of artistic reverie, she felt most herself.

She felt free.

And then she found the tiny frog.

It was far from its habitat beyond the edge of her property which bordered primordial wetlands. A slight incline in the terrain between the water and her sandy gravel driveway posed little challenge for the roving bespeckled stray, who was clinging tenaciously to the side of the fountain basin in a kind of ancient embrace. It saw her and turned stock-still, anticipating attack or capture. But she also turned motionless, and the two locked eyes in a kind of mutual trance that was only broken when she realized the setting sun descending upon them. And so she turned and brought her ink and writing tablet inside for the evening, leaving the diminutive amphibian to his moonlit pleasures.

The next morning, she went looking for him. It was a disappointment when she realized that he was nowhere to be found. Perhaps he was in the fountain reservoir under the fish or back in the primordial marsh waters or under fallen leaves, resting after an evening in her thyme and sage plantings. She wondered if the scent of the herbs gave him as much joy as it did her. But his absence struck her as a metaphor; he was free if not found. And this is how she had seen her own life.

She seated herself and filled her pen with ink. And at that exact moment, a thunderous cracking sound struck overhead.

The front of a great storm began its tear through the trees, knocking out the power. The wind howled and the rain pelted so fiercely that it stung her arms and broke through the dense canopy of swamp maples and hickory, driving a torrent of water into the thirsty soil and forest floor beneath.

She decided to remain conjoined with the chaos of wind and water; it was a tonic to her heart and a curative for her mind.

As the pummel of the driven rain and the fierce air struck her, she saw the frog. He was nestled amongst the stones at the base of the fish, at one with the elements. It made her realize that their existences shared the intensity of being alive in the exquisite presence of nature. As she thought this, he hopped towards the footrest and landed on her naked, wet instep. It felt instantly and simultaneously familiar and foreign, like the touch of a loved friend and a stranger, each wanting whatever physical connection they could grasp. She did not flinch. She wanted to savor this kinship and brave the elements in a duality that neither could have imagined.

They sat with each other for the duration of the storm, she remaining as still as he. The heavy downpour did little to dissuade the frog from remaining steadfast on her foot, and she bore the sting of the heavy rain with a sense of inner resolve and an awareness that her being somehow had become sanctuary.

And then, he leapt in a great show of aerial daring and vanished in the void of the wind and water.

She looked in the direction of his disappearance and felt an overwhelming awe at what had transpired between them. The wonder of it, the elemental forces that intensified the experience, gave her a newfound sense of all that the koi fountain and the stones, the ink and the paper, the sage and the thyme, the wind and the water meant. The grand design was to be found in the stillness of being present for each other. There was nothing greater, above, or beyond.

In the days that followed and the time she now spent writing about her inner awakenings, his presence would come to her at each glance of the koi streaming its cascade of silken splash and her bare feet stepping on the fragrant thyme and the crack of thunder signaling a storm.

She published her first book of short stories; they were about frogs and fountains and swamp maples and a granite Koi fountain that somehow appeared in each vignette. The fountain that had sat for so many decades, overlooked and abandoned, waiting for its destiny as a vessel for its singsong story to be told, allegory for her found purpose, a life of writing.

Her Golden Mean.

Coyote

KANDAKAT-JI, KALIFA THENMOZHI

My hair is cool
So is the air
I run swiftly through the creosote
I smell that smell
Existing nowhere else
Water beckons me
All I need just up ahead
Only a few licks

Across the sandy streets
Sleeping, they are in their homes
Cats meowing their wishes
Me longing for their tender bits
Gato taco dreams

I run, I jump
Leaping in the air with joy
Patches of fur, hoping to be drenched
The ultimate desert rat
Monsoon dreams
The slow pampered dogs
So valued yet always
Always a few paces behind

The sun comes up over the horizon
The dawn breaks with quiet speed
I too must run swiftly
The monsters with two feet
Wiping the grit out of hollowed eyes

Coffee smells wafting through the air
They changed my land
And stole my water
Running through the gulchs
I must run,way from it all

Tomorrow is another day
I am the voice that howls
I am the body that will live
I will survive and outlive them all

UFW - Unsurpassed, Formidable and Worthy

KANDAKAT-JI, KALIFA THENMOZHI

Waving goodbye
Before the dawn
Kids know why
Momma is gone

Layered up
Hat turned down
Prepared to start
Working the ground

Backs bent
Faces brown
Eyes squinting
Looking around

Faces scarved
Hands gloved
Picking crops
That people love

They are here
They belong
We need them
Their days are long

Tender their grasp
Mother's bounty
Picking swiftly
In every county

Grapes and onions
Lemons and limes
Must pick faster
So little time

Thorns say 'no'
Cut through skin
Branches high
Slaps on chin
Stretch and pull
Apple and fig
Guamúchil fruit
Trees laden and big

They are deserving
Humanity runs deep
Natured by Mother
And the crops they reap

From Delano to Sacramento
They went to be heard
Eleven hours daily
Six days preferred

Extreme is heat
Power is here
Together they met
To make it all clear

A life they chose
Maybe so, often not
For this they came
To this very spot

Their eyes cast forward
A dream and a goal
A life well lived
Their actions bold

They're here to stay
They enrich our lives
As they claim their just dreams
Like you and me

Like many before them
Growth through their pain
To hope they all cling
In this, we're the same
They have strength and power
Equality will rise

Home

KNIGHT, KENNADY

If a person is a home,
Then I am a homeless woman, eager to find a home
When I find one, I fall in love, explore every room, and settle in.
Though, every time I get comfortable

Get to know the ins and outs of the house something happens,
It's in someone else's name, pipes break creating a flood, eviction
Then yet again I'm left homeless, alone, and confused
Because as much as I love the house I know I must leave

As much as I want to fix the issue I can't, and if it gets fixed in the future
I will go back and move back in but for now
I will sit with myself no matter the time with the thoughts that I allow
I'm just a homeless woman or a woman without a permanent house.

Public Schools

KNIGHT, KENNADY

On the bus, a familiar rush
At school, the adrenaline flutters, my stomach starts to churn.
Does my mom know I love her?
Do my sisters know I am grateful?

Things I have to think about just in case someone starts loading the clip.
Maybe I looked at them wrong
Maybe we ended on bad terms

How is this a problem and
not everyone's concern?
Worrying about walking through campus to my next class
Wondering if it will be my last.

I get no sleep while I revise what could have gone wrong.
I wandered the halls wondering why it's so hard to belong
Living a life in which i'm stereotyped into a group
Avoiding confrontation, even jumping through hoops

I am so young I should be living not learning about ways to block an intruder
I am only 15. Why am I having this conversation?
Grades and attendance is the priority and expectation
I should be worry about passing, getting my credits
Yet I worry about where to find the nearest exits.

When has this become a norm?
What type of "safety" do we inform
Us kids
Us students should not have to worry about how to stay alive in a place we are supposed
to be Getting an education to become the future of the world.

Flinching on automatic when we hear a bang
Not knowing who to talk to, because they could honestly be in a gang
You report and report and report
You get no support

They hardly do anything even when there are many opportunities.
When will there be peace?
When will people be taken seriously and take a stand
Instead of against a wall or on their knees?

Birthday Song
MARTINEZ, DR. MELINA

Another rotation of the Sun

Five days after most the deeds were done
Marinated in poison
Sliced and stripped
At last, burnt to a crisp

And I am more human than ever
With the year that was the most alive
With such joy and tears
And my body is no longer the same

But I am home at last
And just to feel complete
To the mountain I go

And with each foothold
Painful but with tears of joy
My roots begin to absorb
Nourishment from the soil

Snow melts into my shoes
Water trickles over stones

And I look up to Father Sun
Who never discriminates
We are all equal under his light

I pray I am like Father
And it is then,
My native roots begin to show

The earth gives me grit
Under my broken nails
The grit I need to thrive

Native American, Greek and Roman DNA
Spills at my feet from open wounds

It is my ancestors which come to greet
As their structure mingles with mine

Never before have I felt it till today

It is my blood that I notice
So sharply in my veins

Connecting me to the earth and sky
Clouds and Sun

Strengthening me
Taking me in

Accepting me as theirs
Consuming me into the land
My covenant at last complete

Siberian Ice Maiden
MARTINEZ, DR. MELINA

It brings me great comfort to think of Her
2500 hundred year old Mummy
Laid to rest on the high plateau
    8200 feet- someplace in No-man's land
At the intersection of cultures and peoples
Belonging to everyone and no one at all

Her life, catalogued by burial site,
And Herodotus-
                Trying to make up his mind
Perhaps vacillating
    Between warrior and shaman

With her coriander and cannabis
                3 foot headdress
Felt to the sky
          Axe at her side

Gold leaf jewelry
        The necessities of life

Riding the eastern slopes
        Horse hooves on permafrost

Exposed from under silk blouse,
From the wild worms
            Layered garments
From across the lands
No longer the right size

Six horses sacrificed
Right by her side

The August wind called her cool
With her tattoos
Mythical companions
            On delicate shoulders
Thin from fighting the fight

MRI scans on her restless remains
            Taken from her grave
      Legs softly curled upon her side
Diagnostics, peering inside

Investigation now complete
            Breast cancer into her nodes
And into her bones

From one life to the next
From their dreams into mine
She made it across time
Rising back to life
Being cherished
Being adored
Being loved

The Truth About Survival
MARTINEZ, DR. MELINA

I don't know how

I don't know how
I don't know how to navigate these waters
I can't do this
I can't do that
I'm stuck inside the box
I want out
I want out
My head hits the ceiling
My hands extend and touch both sides
There aren't any holes
I'm no good
I want to be good
More than anything on the planet
I want to please
I don't want to be bad
They squeeze my heart
They burn my hair
They smash my liver
They blister my mouth
They crush my lungs
I'm supposed to like this!!!
It's for a chance
Stop
STOP
Don't stop
I start to hate

Hate

HATE

No, NO

I can't stand me like this

I CAN'T tolerate me

I need relief

This is too painful

The walls are closing in

I'm not allowed to cry

I'm not allowed to scream

I'm not allowed to allow!!!

I'm being watched

Eyes on me

I'm trying so f@%*%#$ hard to fit

I become an animal

Trying to extinguish my needs

Scream

Scream

I can't drink

They will smell it and know

I will set myself back

All my progress gone

I need an outlet

Something invisible

Something that can bring me back

Cut me back to life

Cut me back to calm

I've lost all control

Need to regain

Regain

......

Visualize

Scalpel

I can see it ahead of me

I visualize the steps

Disinfect

Slice
Just one cut
Nice and deep
Gauze
Pressure
Stop the bleeding
But only after I watch it drip
Drip, drip
The satisfaction
The control
To do it properly
To feel the tangible pain
Nothing could hurt more than my heart
I can't want to die
Then I'm truly a bad human
I don't want to be ....
I can't want out
I CAN'T
I have to live
I have to want it
I must

Freight Train Through Phoenix

MATHES, J.D.

After school my brothers and I stood on the electric
box and stared over our safe suburban fence
at the train rumbling west past our house.
We'd count the men sitting in open rail cars, clinging
to the undercarriage, or balancing on the couplings.

The desert sun slanted at hard angles, casting dark
shadows on grimy faces and worn clothes in the folded
blacks and grays of Depression photographs. We boys
imagined riding the rails like heroic vagabonds
in the movies or books. Hobos scrounging for work

in the orchards and fields toward the coasts.
We couldn't imagine the cold bite of steel, the nonstop
vibration shaking their marrow over the miles, over
the days and nights through the relentless wind.
How could we? Kids. Know the cold burn of body heat
lost like the last few dollars spent for a loaf of bread

and a jar of peanut butter, hoping it'll feed him till the next
five dollars. The next seasonal job. We kids couldn't imagine
holding the last sandwich in the heat of a desert day.
Nibbling the crust like it was the last one on Earth.

What did we know of hunger on a freight train, rolling
through Phoenix into a sunset limited by whatever crop
was ripe? To us an empty bread bag caught in the wheels
of a west bound train was just trash, and not
the remnants of some man's last meal.

Venus in Retrograde

MATHES, J.D.

The girls and I drive east,
Sunrise like a creamsicle,
spread only the way a desert
can make it, edged between jagged
mountains and the freezer blue
of a sky, failing before day. The half-light
ripples the frost on the dry lake,
and Venus hangs a punch hole in the dark sky.

We travel to see my father, whose heart
is battered with decades of cigarettes,
industry, and the working-class diet
designed to keep the body burning
through the long shifts of mining ore,
hauling the nation's freight, or the rejection
of a first-born son. The space around
his heart has filled with fluid like so much
sweat and tears of a lifetime of work,
compressing it until it struggles to beat,
to do its job.

My daughters sleep as I drive and regard
Venus through the windshield, fading
with the sunrise. How the son always
feels the pull of the father, no matter
how far away he travels or long ago
the last civil word.
Venus maybe in retrograde,
but it always returns along its frozen
ellipsis, not to the heart, but close enough
to see its light at its brightest.

Healing Scars
MONTOYA, MARIO

The day Magoli came by, I cleaned my studio apartment spotless. I swept, mopped and vacuumed dog hair, lit incense and scrubbed the toilet, inside and out, with Clorox. It looked better, but nothing could wash off the layers of grimy slum that covered my place. Magoli showed up with a bottle of red wine and a camera strapped to her neck. My dog Mia jumped on her as she entered and I apologized. But Mia was no problem, she said. She loved dogs, had a few back home in Las Vegas, New Mexico. I put on *The Girl from Ipanema*, a classic Bossa Nova jazz record. We sipped wine and chatted. I asked her about the camera. Instead of having me pose naked while she painted, she wanted to take photos, as long as I didn't mind. She'd be the only one to see them. Loopy from the wine, I figured, why not? Better than sitting naked for hours.

We polished off the bottle before she asked "Ready?"

I acted confident. "Sure. Let's do this."

I took off my shoe, then my shirt, crumbling with anxiety. I felt skinnier than usual, exposed like a fleshless bone. Magoli encouraged me, so I slid off my khakis. She snapped a few shots. I almost broke into spontaneous shakes. She asked me to remove my underwear. I did as she instructed. I sat there, buttnaked, with only a tube-sock covering my amputated limb. I'd prepped it beforehand, to hide my thickest scar.

"What's the sock for?" she asked.

I shrugged. "I got scars."

"But then you're not nude." She seemed disappointed. "Mind taking it off?"

I hesitated, but I complied, removing the sock. There was no turning back. I felt more exposed without the sock than without boxers, the jagged scar on my limb shaped like the mouth of a grinning shark. If that's what I saw, imagine what she saw. I figured it scared her, grossed her out. But she glanced at it, unfazed, and took a picture, like she'd seen plenty amputated legs. She seemed oddly intrigued.

"Scars are lines on the artwork of our bodies, Mario." Her smile lit my apartment. "They're badges, not blemishes."

Magoli was seeing me for everything I was and wasn't, with nothing, not even clothes, to hide behind. It was nerve-wracking, gut-wrenching, but also exhilarating. Liberating. Me, broken down to my most basic self. She gazed through me, not at me, with a sincere curiosity, reading my scars, searching for the stories they told, and from multiple angles. She took more shots. "Nice. Just relax."

The airflow provided a drafty chill. I felt awkward. "How should I pose?"

"I don't know. Naturally?"

Sensing my nerves, Mia trotted over and sat next to me.

"No, Mia. Get out of the shot," I said.

"No, that's perfect. Let's leave her in a few."

Mia smiled, tongue out, her golden coat shining in the camera. She stole my thunder, soaking up all the attention. But Mia's career as a model only lasted a few shots. She got up and left, more interested in her dogbone.

"Here, let's try this," Magoli said.

She repositioned me in multiple poses. Arms crossed, arms behind me, arms cradling the back of my head. For a few shots, she put me in a pose that resembled *The Thinker*, the famous sculpture, a classic, elegant piece, Magoli told me. She sat me down, elbow braced on my lap, fist holding my chin, mimicking a naked man thinking. Like he was having the deepest, most important thought ever.

"A man in thought or a man struggling on the toilet," I joked.

Magoli laughed. "Hey. Art's serious business."

I made a hard, business face and she giggled. For a moment, I forgot I was naked.

"I got a better idea," she said. "Have any veggies? Like a zucchini?

"I have bananas."

"Ooh. A banana. Perfect."

Magoli sat me down, banana positioned over my crotch, held upright, as she directed. She took photos in successive clicks, turning the camera to achieve different perspectives. She winked and squinted, used her keen, artistic eye to see things in me I never could. Holding myself still was suddenly easier. All the jitters and shame and shaky stiffness had dissolved. For the first time ever, I felt at home in my body, comfortable in my scarred nakedness, fully vulnerable and in front of an attractive woman.

"Don't move," she said. "Those look great."

Healing Scars will appear in a forthcoming memoir by Mario Montoya entitled *The Boy Who Can't Feel*

Lunchtime in The North Valley
MONTOYA, MARIO

You're remembering it like it was yesterday. Singing your ABC's. Stumbling on G. Picking your nose. Noticing fast food signs as they pass left to right in the car window. You recognize your favorite: McDonalds, with its big golden M and its salty golden fries. You can't contain your excitement, yelling as you squirm in your seat belt. "Mom, Mc-Non-olls," you say. "Yes son, I see it." She is gripping the steering wheel, concentrating as she battles traffic. She looks young and slim for twenty-seven, hair hanging off her neck and shoulders. Your grandma sits in the passenger seat, reading the tabloids, relaying the Hollywood chisme to your mom. You don't understand what they're talking about. You're six, one open hand plus a finger.

Outside, the sun is bright as it warms your skin through the glass. Albuquerque looks poor and worn-down, but bustling with people. Bus stops are overcrowded with transients and day-labor commuters, some in orange vests, with gloves and hard-hats. A song comes on the radio that interrupts your ABC's. It's one of your favorites, although you'll regret liking it someday because of its contradicting message. By Neil Diamond, it's called "Coming to America," a fantasy about welcoming immigrants. You like the melodies, although you don't know what it's about yet. Energy builds from sound rushing through you. You can't help but sing along. Your mom increases the volume, cutting your grandma's gossip short. Suddenly you're yelling the words, releasing their power. The simple words, over and over. "They're coming to America. They're coming to America. They're coming to Americaaa. TODAY!"

Your mom sings with you, but your grandma rolls her eyes. You both continue. You're having so much fun. And at that moment, it's all you know about freedom. The freedom to yell "TODAY" as loud as you possibly can.

Then, the music's over. The freedom stops dead in its tracks. Red brake-lights glow as cars honk, skidding to a halt. Your mom reaches back, holding you safe in your seat. A man in a black coat and beanie runs across a busy intersection. He's holding what looks like a sack of potatoes, or maybe money. Someone in a blue uniform is chasing him with a chrome handgun. At first, you think it's a toy. He yells "Stop!" but the other man doesn't obey, stumbling up a highway embankment, out of breath like he's been sprinting for blocks and blocks. The armed man stops and takes steady aim, making sure he's accurate. The world around him becomes still.

Bam.

The sudden shot echoes off the concrete overpass. All is silent, even car horns go mute. The man with the sack hits the floor like he's only beanie and bones. He lays there, motionless, until gravity takes a hold of his body, dragging him down the concrete slope. A trail of blood follows. The man with the gun inspects the limp corpse, his eyes widened with terror, his gun drawn and shaking, still taking aim.

"Mom, what's going on?" you ask, tears building inside your throat. She reaches back again, to cover your eyes with her hands. But you can still see through the space in between her fingers.

"Nothing hito," she says. "Everything's fine."

Somehow you know she's not being honest. Not completely.

"Mom. Here," she says to my grandma. "Cover his eyes while I drive. I'll get us out of this mess."

Your mom maneuvers around dense traffic, avoiding vehicles as she escapes. Your grandma blocks the scene with the palm of her hands. But you can still see the man on the floor through the cracks in her arthritic fingers, blood pooling, drowning what's left of your innocence.

You never receive an explanation. You go home and take a nap, like everything's normal. But nothing is normal ever again. You know what happened was real and not a movie. And you have lifelong nightmares of a man chasing you and putting a gun to your head. You feel the cold steel against the bend of your neck, but the faceless man never pulls the trigger before you wake, heart throbbing through your veins. You don't understand why he never kills you. But you do know a crippling fear overwhelms you at night. And that for years and years into adulthood, you'll never trust a cop again.

Lunchtime in the North Valley was published in *All at Once I Saw My Colors* (2017), an anthology by Z Publishing House

Body as Self Ceremony
MUÑOZ, BRIANA

I take inventory.

My fingers,
        instruments for writing poems
Poems that gracefully attack, against fascism,
                  against the war

My elbows,
at dinner, I question who invented table manners
discover
        this as a class construct

"Discover" tastes in my mouth like "Conquest"

Breasts,

Western culture teaches me to have breasts is
to be a devil,
     temptress,
     mujer sin verguenza
     taboo from birth
Birth awakens the ducts to flow
liquid gold into the innocence of my baby

Everything about my breasts is natural
Nature is sacred
Therefore, I am.

My navel, life source, phantom limb, center of my vessel
I mourn the placenta that was separated from me

thirty years ago

"Physician" tastes in my mouth like "Wary"

My ancestors knew this. Modern society grows wary of traditional medicine.
Tastes in my mouth like big fuckin' pharma

Pelvis, holy sacrum, cervix,
Útero, clitoris, clítoris, clitoride,
klitoris,
maybe if I spell it in every language
        they (men) will find it

"Clitoris" tastes in my mouth like "ceremony"

Thighs disguised as mini skirt attraction
Dictionary
at·trac·tion
a place which draws visitors by providing something of interest or pleasure:
"the church is the town's main tourist attraction"

thighs built to climb Teotihuacán temples
My body, city of the Gods, the most holy land
sunrise ceremony dedicated to the breath I am allowed
every day.

Piñon Saga
ORTIZ, CHRISTIANNA

Earth, water, wind, fire

Knowledge, wisdom, heart, power

Nature's perennial muse

Renacimiento

ORTIZ, CHRISTIANNA

Invisible ache

Wild hope

Forgiven moments in hue of blue

Iridescent you

Serene, sacred badlands

Black crow, wise spirit guide

Omen of change

Magical Totem

Soul soaring between two worlds

Journeys of a lifetime represented in the hollows of one's heart

Alluvial bajadas

Picturesque wilderness, fantastic and wild

Beautiful ruins of becoming

Blood is Land

ORTIZ, RONNIE

Mi tierra sangre
It was a beautiful summer to fall day
Under the skies that cradled my Grandma
between sacred hills and farm land near El Rio'

We were excited to celebrate!
Present for my co-madres who couldn't be
Yet we said too soon: conquistador stupidity,
Not today...

Upon arrival to the party
it felt like danger – there was a creep. in a red hat
He was filming & stalking the women
Just another spawn of hate being stupid

I got wary and wore a mask
It's what I needed to do.
How could I manage thru being targeted?
My friends had already been exposed... Dios mio...

No one really expected filthy shit on site
I wasn't ready for this, we weren't
More than just desecration
Theres was enacted as a means to instigate

We tolerated the invasive behaviors
and the Desgraciados who would eat our food!
breaking bread in the morning!
Desgraciados!!!

Puro movida they formed alliances with magats
Signalling guns & stating cruelty against even young children
Desgraciados who sell out their kin and neighbors
To grab power cause they're fading away
We weren't ready for back stabbers, liars, nor evil
We had Love, Prayers, Celebration
FRESH TORTILLAS!!! and fancy coffee
were on our tongues

#WeWillBeHeard
was the only middle ground moment outside of joy
Beautiful faces, kids playing, and
Saya feeding people

It was so pretty outside
in the llano...
We should have sang and danced
...but we didn't get the chance.

Fool started pressing towards the center
Trying to rush towards the woman leaders
The men wanted to protect us
n videos going everywhere to catch it all for history

Aaauuuuughhhhh!!!!!!!!

I had forgot to scream with everyone else
(Later messenger Aaron screamed Free Palestine from within the flames)

When I asked Mohammad, our Palestinian guest,
He said this was bad (from what he'd thus seen)
Ohhhh, had we known then...
We would have sung "from the river to the sea"

If anyone else had been shot,
few would have cared
More like blamed us for our voices and moving feet
But Jacob almost didn't come back to life that day

And later when the shock of invaders wore off
Our community has a hero, a Backbone for us & the earth
Prayers protected young hermanita
Jacob's prayers saved us all ~ Strong and Beautiful

Blood is Land, ~En Memoriam~, Feb. 2024 on YouTube

Chicanos del Norte

ORTIZ, RONNIE

I wish Crazy Jack had <u>never</u> sold
    the field of giant, wild sunflowers

That changed everything

A wall was built
        and after Grandma died,
   You couldn't walk all easy to Connie's no more

The sold land   well, they put in a gas tank
  to leak into the ground
                  No more eating roses
  and making peach-leaf mud-pie tacos

Nov. 3 ~ Tio Franke's anniversary
            puro Casados se murio

  I used to wonder if my family worked at the brick pinta
Yeah, but they also had a butcher shop downtown

Prima Luisa Dora   used to be Loud
  It's cause you have to be at the ranch

       Butterscotch candies   -   Safeway
   and Uncle Ralph's '55 Chevy - stock
he looked like great Fernando Lopez   del Norte
   hands so big   backhand would take criminales out

What happened to everybody?
   The cops shot neighbor Lopez at the courthouse

Still roams around   - Someone I met had heard him
    I let her know he was always good to me

Truth was truth
    Bullshit got called out
But no familia lives in Grandma's house
    some extrajeno with no idea

Blood is land

los Sangre de Chistos tambien
but the ski basin pours out the propaganda
        with the rest of their waste water

Hito Lindo I hope you'll feel things
    like they used to be
more soul than any product
    could ever be

Chicanos del Norte
            and where are we now?
Tijerina and the Guadalupe Hidalgo Treaty

Maybe that's why we can't sell out

Malcolm X said it well – by any means necessary
        Indios have gambling now
They're sovereign – but the government
    still keeps Leonard Peltier

    My soul may be tired
        but what's up?
La gente's gotta take care of themselves

        And I've cried a million star-lit nights
The big window in the Snail house
    n the choo-choo to Cerrillos
I still hear loud   como la Tasha, my wolf-dog

But I'm glad old Frenchy's Field
        stayed full of flowers

Communication to the people
        Walk with a pure heart
    and sparkling blue eyes like Tio Tomas

Flamenco dancers in the sky
        could I be a curendera someday?
home in El Norte   THIS land I Love

Chicanos del Norte read at Alas de Aqua exhibition Aug 2022

Prayer for Freedom
ORTIZ, RONNIE

Ohhhhh   Ohhhhh

...

This a prayer for an is old man
This a prayer for the children
This a prayer for the Indigene
Please set them free

Behind the walls
In jail cells
On cold floors
with starless nights

Sit the Innocent
Sad – and – lost
Torn from the Earth
of Turtle Island

The system would have U believe
< but no >   it's wrong –
Cause policing's based on slave catching
Slaving based on white supremacy
And Manifest Destiny
        Imperialistic, capitalistic, indoctrination
Got U believin' in society 'bout
material wealth not health
bout military glory not Love –

It's time our relatives   not migrants

Came back to <u>ancestral</u> <u>lands</u>
And I dream
of Leonard Peltier being home

Prayer for Freedom presented at the International Museum of Folk Art, July 2023

Baskets

PHOENIX, NADINE RACHEL

Dedicated to a loved one and mothers who have lost a child.

In the intricate tapestry of my daily life, the number twenty-seven weaves its way relentlessly. Once, fresh memories hung to dry over two decades, yet still fresh in my mind, as if time forgot to age that instance. Aged, dried, and left out for years so healing wouldn't shrink or lose shape when the time came to create. It materializes subtly yet persistently, gracing the facades of buildings as North 1027, a delicate dance at 10:27 on clocks, twice, and even unveiling itself as I prepare the nourishment that my body needs to get through this on the analog above the sweltering stove.

The omnipresent recurrence of 1027 has become an inescapable companion, searing its mark upon mundane routines and sentimental moments. When prompted, it holds the key to my belongings — "Enter a code you will remember." Punching the numbers 1-0-2-7. These numbers echo the weight of over two decades' worth of loss.

These digits, seemingly innocent and meaningless to most, have transformed into a lasting symbol, a haunting reminder etched into the fabric of my existence. They stand as keepers of the past, guardians of what was never, and the enduring echo of a story written in the language of numbers. A story only known by me, carried by me. Every single day, for half of my life.

The ground freezes over; new life begins, and the sunbeams from the clear skies and then right back again to a moment in time where all five senses are flooded. When the leaves begin to fall again. The numbers are now accompanied by Autumn for the end-of-the-year concert. A celebration of life and accomplishments, losses, successes, beginnings, and endings. A time to gather and reminisce with loved ones and new and old friends. Pumpkins radiating with their orange hues like trumpets blaring through the sounds of the percussion, red leaves, staccato among the greens, yellow squash accenting as loud crashes with a harmonic profile, browns are the deep basses, the beat, the rhythm of the daily moments that keep moving along. Cinnamon, Cardamon, and ginger are all reminders of family, connectedness, love, joy, and warmth. A beautiful time for most, some of us, a time of pain, loss, and suffering.

Each year, many sticks are produced ranging in thickness, suitable for different parts of healing and growth. Some thin, some thick, all important in rebuilding the foundation that was shattered. It's advisable to use a therapist for this journey. Reminders that the thicker parts are good for the base, and the thin ones, the weavers, should be left for structure. For the areas that don't need too much support. Order number 1027, logged on at 10:27 p.m., crossing the finish line at 10:27:01.

Sorting the years into two separate piles of sticks. The thick pile and the thin pile. Drawing upon each pile. Additional sessions were held to ensure a sufficient number of sticks to choose from. Doubling the amounts would also offer security and comfort, the therapist said. There will always be more projects because there will always be more projects.

Begin with the slath. Take 4 of the thickest sticks from the sessions where a great deal of introspection, crying, and purging occurred. The ones that had the greatest catharsis. These will be used for the base; cut them to the appropriate size. Now, split half of the sticks. Don't worry; progress is not lost, for splitting is required at each center.

Use the knife carefully, working the middle by turning the blade to open the split and thread the four non-split sticks through to form the slath. The sticks are not all uniform; some ends are thicker than the others. Some sessions took longer to process, which were thinned and drawn out. Some sessions ended abruptly because clarity was achieved and progress was made, so the ends are a bit thicker. Alternating the thick and thin ends to balance things out may be a good idea.

Weave the base with a pairing weave. Begin clockwise around each of the four arms of the slath. Make sure to hold it tightly together, as each stick took a great deal of time to create. Find the two longest and thinnest sticks to use as the weavers; remember the ones that took the longest to process, the ones where progress was stagnant for months on end. The protracted evenings were accompanied by drool-covered pillows, persistent panic attacks, and uncontrollable crying fits. Use those and trim a few inches off the ends that are a bit damaged and straggly. Some sessions were tough and not every session was perfect. Insert the tips into the slath and position the weaver between the next arm, bring it back up and over the next arm, and keep the top weaver down behind. Do it again; the therapist is here in case you have questions. For the next arm, bring the weaver from the backup and over and the top weaver down behind. Rotate the slath counterclockwise to keep the handling the same with each stroke. Pull the weavers tightly as you go, a gentle reminder, as one already knows. Each stick is treasured and cherished, a testament to the work that was done. Treated with caution.

Continue to weave, a nice steady rhythm. But now weave between each individual slath stick. Instead of four, there are now 16. Each now has a separate arm, just like before, only more. Bend each set of 4 sticks as you reach them to form spaces like the spokes of a fan. Remember to be firm and get things tight and close. These sticks are strong; hours of work go into each one, pull firmly with every move, removing every gap as it is weaved, too far in, and it will be impossible to remove any gaps. This is a slow and carefully crafted process. Take your time.

Weave around and around, splicing in new weavers along the one already added. This will take time; the base must be crowned and strong, it can be flat if one chooses. Let's keep it crowned the first time because there will be occasions when flat ones are required. We need a strong base right now, and crowning it will make it stronger. Continue weaving the base until there is a solid foundation. Make it big or small. You get to choose; this is for you.

Thread in each moment, each triumph, each setback as you rotate the base. Finish with tip ends and lock them off with one more weaver. Each building upon the next, holding one another in place. Bring all the healing together. One by one.

Thread the next weaver between previous rows to keep the ends held in. The ends of the weavers should be cut but still rest against a spoke to ensure they don't stick out on the other side of the base. You can keep the cut pieces for another time or toss them as they serve no other purpose. The base is complete; don't worry if it doesn't look neat; this is the first time. Be kind to yourself, and don't lose hope.

Numerous baskets in different sizes will be crafted throughout time. Sufficient to store the Fall harvest every year. Combining the recent and historical. Cradling the memories of the present and the past with each passing year. All entwined, upheld, and formed into a single, distinctive piece. There will be an abundance to distribute eventually. Keep the first one close as a reminder that although the mending process started off ragged and difficult, it will eventually become polished and seamless.

Twenty-two years since the creation of the first stick.
Ten baskets were made, and 27 were given away.
2001 will be made this lifetime.

Echoes of Resilience - A Symphony of Abusive Love and Life

PHOENIX, NADINE RACHEL

My weary backside bears the weight of existence. Each strike is a testament to the battles lost. Hands calloused from the trials they've endured, marked by resilience, etched with stories untold. In the ebb and flow of breath, life persists. A reminder of the fragile beauty of existence. With every inhalation, the universe whispers, granting solace and strength to carry on. Tears cascade down an unstoppable river. Sobs wrack my body, releasing the pain within. A cathartic outpouring, a cleansing of the soul. Each drop is a testament to the depth of emotion. Amidst the tempest of emotions, I am alive. My heart was beating with fervor, blood coursing through my veins. A resounding affirmation of my earthly presence and a reminder of the infinite possibilities that lie ahead. In this shared existence, you, too, are alive. A precious soul, a vessel of untapped potential. Bathed in the radiance of life's boundless energy, navigating the world with innocence and wonder. The potential is lost, hidden under addiction and pain. Does he love me? A question that lingers. The uncertainty pierced through the depths of my being. Yet, amidst the doubt, he chose to let me live. Then it must be true, for I am here, heartbeat still pulsing. A testament to a love that defies comprehension. Calmness descends a gentle whisper in the chaos. Guiding me to find peace within the storm. Reveling in the stillness, finding solace. Allowing the wounds to heal and scars to fade. Does she love me? The silence speaks volumes. An unspoken language, pregnant with meaning. Yet, in the absence of words, love can manifest. In the subtlest of gestures, in a tender touch. But receiving these small acts paralyzes her. She was not taught to love but taught to fight. Navigating life, survival at the forefront, escaping incest and molestation. Love for her was in the form of providing a much better environment for her children. Even though it lacked apparent love, for her, this was love.

Rocking back and forth, self-soothing rhythms entwined. A gentle sway to calm restless thoughts. Alone because mothers holding sad children only existed on TV. In the cradle of night, finding solace and peace. Alone because our people were taught to be tough. Embracing the comfort of dreams' tender embrace. The only way to escape loneliness is to dream a dream where I am loved and held. Regret lingers, haunting my thoughts. The weight of past mistakes is pressing upon my conscience. How much regret can a child have? A whispered reminder that I have faltered. Yet, even in imperfection, I find my humanity. I am human, flawed, and vulnerable. Not a decade has passed on this earth when thoughts of suicide appear, but you can't see that even when made explicitly clear. Navigating the labyrinth of existence with uncertainty. Thoughts not of toys and imaginative play but of calculation, survival, and avoidance. Yet resilient, capable of growth and redemption, forging my path through trials and tribulations. Knowing that this is not forever, You, my dear child, are in the bloom of youth. A flower yet to fully unfurl its petals. Radiating innocence, curiosity, and boundless potential. A testament to the wonders of life's continuous cycle. The sting of my hand lingers—a painful reminder of the consequences of youthful choices made and lessons learned. A poignant reminder that wisdom often comes at a cost. Etching the boundaries of right and wrong into my consciousness. It is too early to protest, for my existence is at stake. In the palm of your calloused hands, subconsciously whisper to me, "You should have known better." A gentle reproach echoed through the chambers of my youthful mind. Yet, within the realm of mistakes lies wisdom's seed. A catalyst for growth and transformation. As my heart aches with the weight of life's burdens. What does life have to offer if it is already difficult to bear? Each beating is a testament to the depths of emotion. Love morphs into hate. For he is not worthy of my love. I will pretend to love and become a pathological liar. Love courses through my veins, an eternal flame. Nurturing resilience, igniting the spirit's resilience. I am alive, a beacon of vitality and strength. Embodied in the ebb and flow of breath. As you, my dear child, continue to grow. Unfurling your wings, embracing the world's wonders. My weary eyes burn from the weight of tears shed. Yet, within the depths, a spark of resilience glimmers. For in every tear lies a reservoir of strength. A testament to the capacity to endure and overcome. Within the safety of this sacred space, from within, I find solace. Shielded from the tempests that rage outside. Love's warm embrace encircles, providing sanctuary. A gentle reminder that I am held, I am protected. My reality, my choice.

Fatigue settles in, a weariness that permeates. Yet, within the weariness, a quiet strength resides. For even in exhaustion's grasp, love's flame endures. Guiding me forward, lighting the path ahead. He is asleep now, finding a respite in the slumber's embrace. His presence never soothes my weary soul. In the realm of dreams, love's whispers persist. Yet, it falls on his deaf ears. Tying us together in the tapestry of shared existence. Too young to escape, too weak to fight back. Love, a constant companion, is ever-present within. Flowing through the veins of our shared journey. Pulsing through my veins, muddled in his. A lifeline that sustains, nurtures, and uplifts. A guiding force that weaves its magic throughout our lives. But he can't hear it; I, only a child, can feel it. I wish he did, too.

The Struggle for Identity and Belief

PHOENIX, NADINE RACHEL

Born into a world where the hue of my skin is the gauge of my value and my gender assumes an inferior status, I exist to serve—destined to labor for others, tasked with uplifting their self-worth. I am a benchmark to measure against when the majority seeks an ego boost, a target for those who feel I am overachieving; I must know my place. Hope dwindled early, before comprehension began before I knew the identity of a brown girl, a brown woman, a brown human. In a society where hostility towards melanin prevails as the norm, I, a mere child, faced a fate measured by brown paper bags. Success is determined by passing, akin to winning the lottery for an unscathed existence. Luck lies in hues of high yellow, hovering on the verge of becoming too dark if too much time is spent under the sun. Redbone is not quite the pleasing shade for discerning eyes. A shade that falls just shy of being light enough but is almost too dark. A precarious balance on the cusp of what might have been, with just a touch more privilege, insufficient to foster self-belief or secure a leadership position. It allows one enough freedom to stand on the fragile glass edge, only to be nudged off before reaching the glass ceiling and breaking through.

Mountain

RAFF, IVY

I never axe-chopped any man in a shirt who carted off my children, called them
lumber. I never stuck sharp-tip poles in skins of campers, nor stuffed the dynamite
back in miners' throats. You can keep it all. I live for the slow blank bristle

of every day. I live for the lover who sees the outline of me against gunmetal skies
of November & doesn't seek to own me. Soon the creatures on my spines
will calm their skittishness, lose memories of hunting rifles, assemble

forever-nests for their babies. Soon brown bears will return
to paw my rivers for salmon & beavers will rebuild dams. I remember
those old fertile days. I remember them all the way from my beaten soils

to my summit's mica glint. I remember them from brontosauri, woolly mammoth,
all the shimmer of water phyla across geologic time scales, fossil-imprint
clamshells in shale. I remember the sea blanketed me each night

for sixty thousand millennia. Do you remember your mother? I remember
when this place was an ocean & my peak was a baby, an island, a speck.
I remember being a rock. Old as the hills, goes your expression - honey, you don't

know the half. You reach inside me & find copper. But it's mine, that mine
you think is yours. My life is to grow iron inside. I need it
there more than you need your armor, your autos. My life is to live after

you've taken all that's mine, after you've cleared my forest & picked my fruit.
My truth is regeneration your poets can't rhyme, your music can't sing.
My lover is the wind. My first child you call dirt & devalue. My life

you reduce to aluminum, but when you're gone the wind will sing me celebration,
touch me soft, let my metals rest. My places are sacred. In the end
you won't have them. Keep looking up at me,

not because I hold your answers but because hell will ring at your bones
if you forget. My life is to do Nothing. Nothing in the wake of your penetrations.
You call me a mountain. I call myself nameless, majestic as the g?d

Jews won't pronounce. My life's pocked with caves. Come for a sit. Taste what it is
to be mountains, find space in your ribs. Find give in your spine. Find
your porous nature at my granite face. My life needs no words - it's beyond
this Time. My life is to sit. My lover kicks up or dies, that ephemeral wind.
My life is to wait for him, greet him still when he comes. Yearn with no passion,
permanent peace. I comfort the stars, never envy their burning.

Nothing Compares
RAFF, IVY

Eyes of October's Irish Sea – all temperatures at once.

I was too young for a love like that but her vocals carved a gorge. Today I accept the bottomless well: I may not see the love I think I need during this collection of breaths I call a life.

○

In my early twenties I lived in a dirty tenement in Hell's Kitchen. Single handedly populated the ground floor's karaoke bar with musician friends.   Every week I nagged Mary Hanley to do "Nothing Compares 2 U." It never wore. No matter what drunken hookups or brawls brewed, everyone silenced when Mary inhabited Sinéad. Mary - wisp of fairy Goth-daughter, smeared Merlot lipstick, too-thick eyeliner, torn fishnets. When she sang that song she was an angel.

Sinéad refused to perform sexuality and allure. Karen Finley asked me, *How do you relate to that?* I said, *With the same admiration I hold for mountain climbers & others who achieve what I will never.* I stand on my little bound feet, mirror-check several times a day, ensure this dress lays properly over my silhouette, my hair curls according to my will. I do not know whether femininity was born in me like the propensity for freckles, or beaten into me like the lie that screamed at the inner walls of my skull this morning when I secured the door shut behind my new man. *He can't get away from you fast enough.*

○

I would be an awkward colt with a shaved head. In my feedbag gather a thousand grains that taste like the Stanley Steemer carpet cleaning tech telling me he wants to rub my pretty toes. He'd knelt on the floor to show me where old glass chips buried in the padding. Men's desires: gardens I tend. Fat red bell peppers slice open, reveal flat white seeds.

○

After Norman's death, my grandmother lamented in my arms, *What is a woman's life if there is no husband to need her?*

I pen achievable action plans every day. I need written-out structures. Else I hack at my arms with shards of funhouse mirrors.

○

My mother was – is – weak in her constitution. I grit sand on her soft pink tongue, never turn pearl. She hardly breathes around me, much less sings her violin's long plaintive cries. Mine drowns hers. When I was young she locked me where walls would absorb my sound. This is common in addict households. She feared kicking the wasp nest of my father's habit, doused her daughter in pesticides instead. Her eyes reside at the geographic center of a billowing white tent.

This is what I inherit from my family: lemming-like desires to numb. I never called it that. I called it pleasure, rocketed to the one place I didn't have to think about how small my world had become. How, in that cold corner of Michigan, in a whole week the only human voice I heard was my own addict husband's.

○

I'm not for this public. They're not for me. I fantasize about the year 2183, a century from my death. Advanced humans unclasp their UV protection suits to kiss into each other's mouths potable water infused with my microchipped poetry. That's how I want them to transmit me, via love to which nothing compares.

○

I harbor the harmed. No longer a fighter, nor a brawler. I fought for the better part of my life. No one's lot improved for it, least of all mine. I shelter the damned, as Sinéad did. Good days come one at a time.

Noble life is to sit, quiet. Let your death take its time. Wade in the sea. Watch sunlight on its ripple.

the Artist called

RAFF, IVY

g?d crafted sparrows & their sycamores.
one purple midnight the sparrows
loosed songs as irises unfolded,
my legs violin strings in the photosynthetic
hands of a man the Artist sent me.

they never sing at night, the man
whispered. *isn't that odd?* & as his body closed
over mine, they silenced. all night
he moved forward, a wave
that never reached shore, never longed for shore.
sparrows, sky-spined, know nothing of floods like this,
though their evolution warned them
its depth. after their serenade
they left the winds of their spot-lungs to trail, drown
in fragile bells of ribs. drifted to sycamore
sleep while the man & i whipped gales:
atlantic.

Chicano Hickey

REY, MANNY

Secretive glances and sexual urges
Culminate at the end of the night with a rite of passage.
Some lustful types or wannabe vampires
Will fall prey with a bite on the neck.
A badge of courage, or far worse, a hickey.
A modern-day scarlet letter
Stamped, marked, or tagged
By an ambitious, rogue, and Banksy-type artist paramour
That prays to paint on a delicate skin canvas.
Painted on by kissing lips that suck
From a palette mixed with paints
Tinged with tones of lust and passion.

Sensual art hangs from her neck
Showcasing a collection on full display
Peeking out of necklines
Born from a make out session,
That teeters on the precipice of sex and sin
In the front seat of my car
Is how the night ended.

My mamasita,
My sexual sanctuary,
My ruca lets me paint her neck
Every time my hyna loca
Leans back to reveal her trust and fragility,
As I swoop down to her soft nape
And suck on her my latest creation titled, Chupada y Marcada
On her bare gallery walls
A love tattoo, black and blue necktie, monkey bite, or chupeton.

A passionate moment snapshot,
Splashed on her neck for all to see,
From her pinchi vampire lover
That sucks lust rather than blood.

The Bosque Cries

REY, MANNY

The Rio Grande
Heart of the Mesilla Valley
One of nature's prized crowns and inlaid by a precious gem,
Water—once bountiful,
Crested along the banks in a glorified pageantry of fluid flow.
Pomp and circumstance on full display.

Ay Rio Grande,
Everyone that gazed at your beauty
Stood by with adoration to watch nature's parade
Unfold and flow gently down the stream.
Merrily, merrily, life was but a dream.
And in this dream, the river's open vein
Carried healing waters of hopes and dreams,
Until intense heat and seasons of drought and doubt
Scorched the land and stole the waters,
Leaving back only a trickle of what once was
To meander through pencil thin pathways
Permitted by and for the amusement of the unrelenting sequía.

Rio Grande, stripped of its grandness,
Resorts now traverse a course as a trivial tributary.
Your skin, a desiccated channel,
Stiffens more and more with time.
Taut and parched sand bars
Strangle and suffocate the river to give in,
And surrender to its fate,
As the Rio goes belly up to reveal its chapped underbelly.

Worry not old river, for you are not alone.
At the edge of your existence and straddling your fringe,
Majestic and imposing rows of cottonwood trees
Stand guard and salute you with deference.
They offer their sympathy, love, and loyalty,
Through remembrance and lamentation.
These devoted champions of the Bosque
Burrow their roots deep into your banks
In search of secluded brackish water
Seasoned with the tears of all that wail for you.

Rio Grande of mine,
Nature is wise and understands the circle of life,
For the brooks, streams, and arroyos
Eagerly await the return of cyclical waters.
A celebration of new beginnings
Heralds in days of wine and roses
When the heavens douse the land with fruitful rains
To recharge and restore your former glory.

Grande Rio, the unwavering and resolute cottonwood trees
Will stand guard and be by your side.
Like sentries,
These enormous trees will stand at their post,
Holding the line and guarding the Rio's borders
Waiting on the firmament between life and death
To protect and provide much needed shelter and refuge,
And save what's left of the Rio Grande.
The fertile soils on top of your banks
Will be a birthplace,
So that saplings can grow to be pinchis arbolotes.
Monstrous towers of bark reaching high
To pierce the turquoise sky in hopes of stealing a precipitated kiss,
As their silver dollar scalloped leaves snap and dance to the slightest breeze,
From a song sung by the desert wind's gentle hiss.

The little saplings will grow to stretch their limbs to the clouds,
And reach for the stars,
Rising high like Shaquille O'Neal
To block the sun's shot,
And give us ground dwellers a lot
Of cool and dappled shade
That waits for the rains to return and revive the Rio Grande's majesty.

Keep the faith grand river,
For the day will come
When the nourishing waters our forefathers spoke of
Return with a growl and a heaping bounty of liquid gold,
To climb your banks and rest on a perch
Ready to crest over your earthen lips.

But until that day comes,
The Bosque cries.

Always with You

ROYBAL, RONALDO

I love you gramma, my sweet friend
What is it like to be a spirit?
Do you still wear your wispy cotton dresses
tattered and so soft and thin from the years of living?

Your room next to ours without a closet
the only time your daily dresses were hung
was while they were on the clothesline
dancing in the soft desert wind
with your sweet touch you pinched open the clothespins
you gathered your clothes in your thin arms
they all managed to fit loosely in your small dresser

Do spirits miss the taste of cigarettes?
the ritual of breathing through the small blazes
you would sometimes put your cigarettes out on your dresses
I always noticed things like that about you
you always seemed more comfortable with imperfection

Thin cotton dresses with cigarette burn holes
sometimes you would hold my hand while we walked
in the desert foothills looking for herbs
your boney hands, swollen from rheumatoid arthritis
yucca, osha root and chimajá gathered in your dress

Do spirits laugh?
Does my packaged way of life seem funny to you?
Can we walk together again someday gramma?

"Mi jito I'm always with you."

Freddy Won't Eat at *Tomasitas*

ROYBAL, RONALDO

Freddy Roybal won't eat at *Tomasitas*
when we go out to order their stuffed *sopaipillas*
he stays back at home for my mom's *calabacitas*
yet we order blue plates with blue corn *tortillas*

But still, Freddy won't eat at *Tomasitas*
he loves his beans and *chile* with homemade *tortillas*
and discussing the water with *tíos* and *tías*
while gramma does dishes and makes him *natillas*

He works all day hoeing his rows of *chile*
then yells to me "I'm watering tomorrow, *dile*!"
"And why go for what I can eat at home, *cabrones*!"
he'd rather stay home for his own *chicharrones*

He might grill some lamb chops from his own *borreguitas*
while my brother and I order fresh *margaritas*
he'll drink homemade wine and forego their *sangrias*
because Freddy Roybal won't have dinner at *Tomasitas*

The New Mexican Madman Dressed in Business Casual

ROYBAL, RONALDO

The New Mexican Madman wakes up with the sunrise
still half asleep, a cosmic glaze in his eyes
his mind reels with visions and hopes from his dreams
a kaleidoscope bath of ethereal scenes

His breakfast *tortillas* wrap green *chile picante*
the New Mexican madman steps out of his *chante*
he tucks in his shirt and he adjusts his tie
he feels like a *cabrón* in this *pinche* disguise

His inbox is filled with exclamations in the subject
his *pantalones* confess a Banana Republic
his blood pumps from guzzles of Starbucks caffeine
he makes personal use of the copy machine

This slow corporate death seems agonizingly gradual
for a New Mexican madman dressed in business casual

Enchanted - Mother Earth and Sister Sky

SANCHEZ, STACIE L.

The sun sets across the land.
The trees lengthen under the shadows
Of the moon and the stars.
The sky, now a curtain. Dark.

The Milky Way smiles wide against the mid-night blue.
The moon dimples my Sister-Sky's cheek.
My land. Enchanting from any view,
But this mesa was my gift just for her.

She is the Keeper of the stars and moon,
The stargazers, the Star lovers,
And the vast desert above the creek.

Lending herself, her comfort, to the audience
Who gawks her show, night, by night, by day.
Hoping, praying to understand
Her secrets above.

Below the edge of the swollen water run.
Steady and lulling. It's magic scoring, reflecting the desert night.
Light, by day, the visitors abandon their oven shelf, their mesa bed.
To cross the water and mingle and dance with me, my trees.

As it mixes, the breeze, cooling air, desert heat.
The fish awaken, the visitors eat, and the does arrive.
Then quickly retreat.
The visitors play under the shade. Then they nap at my bank,
As poles rest patiently, and calm, for a nudge from our other sister, the stream.

Mostly all is still from the desert' atmosphere,
With strict exception of the Indian Breeze, wrapping itself round and around,
Every bend and every twig, while it chases off the ghosts of the day.
Upon the shelf, where the campers sleep, the breeze picks up to a mild wind.

Gusting with heat across the land. Flirting with cactus and sand, fighting.
But soon, again the sun resides low, taking with it a hot wind-tide.
Leaving the visitors to enjoy once more the magic show,
Of my sister, and her enchanting desert night sky

Together
SANCHEZ, STACIE L.

In the garden we invent our dance.
The scent of roses,
      intoxication
      hallucination

We hover
with the dragon flies,
Above the pool, dark, with romance

Here we fly Free, Free of this disease.
Our hearts filled with fire, passion of life,
      love
      desire

To be of the future
We absorb the sun,
      the shine,
      imbibe

Clasp our hands together
Building the energy to cope.
No need to leave our garden.
Where we thrive
With the goddess of hope

10PM. Stopped. Frisked.

WELLINGTON, DARRYL LORENZO

One Man cries *I Am I am*
    in ecstasy and terror   *I Am*
as the Lord cried
    to Moses. Three men
dressed in monochrome
    and camouflage
faces hardened
    decline to listen
ignoring a strangled plea
    descended from a timeless
sensibility behind
    compassionate justice and
ritual prophesy. A nearby
    parking meter winks
casts an arbitrary
    light on an asphalt
street corner. Witnesses
    nothing. Glitters
after dark. Stands
    like a watch-
tower going senile
    totteringly decadent
on duty to collect
    poised to pinch
the nickels and dimes
    the irrevocable fines
the regular tariffs
    the evidence requisite
blind to other charges of citizenship.

Lady of Sweeter Justice
WELLINGTON, DARRYL LORENZO

The thumbs turned. The fists gripped.
The sky blanched. The chains kindled.
The links severed. When the aroma
dazzled the expectant workers, dazed
sandaled checkers at retail shopping centers,
stunned the noses of horticulturalists
who presumed a fertile and overzealous
spring mischievously excited local color
schemes crying *if this sweet oil exists,*
peace, justice and spirit was an opiate.

And looking back on it, all
the sighs of *Amen* and *ahem*
from the distance of many eons
with the impartiality of a scholar,
no one honestly suspected,
nobody knew to agree
before the turn of North winds South,
and the white robes billowing, a shaky
pan splashed distilled perfumes,
before the gardeners lightly, whimsically,
lifted blank gazes and smiled, *given this,*
peace, justice and spirit was an opiate.

Lady of Sweeter Justice, originally published in the collection *Legible Walls*
Stalking Horse Press, 2023

The Identity Closet

WELLINGTON, DARRYL LORENZO

A face wants to be a carnival mirror.
A mirror wants an average face.
Secrets, hidden, subtly keyed.
Nuances never left behind.
Nothing matters like everything long past.
Personae. Not revealed, nor eschewed.
Duality is a narrow hiding place

Biographies
Artists, Authors and Poets

VICTORIA ADAMS

Contact: cdicfo@comcast.net | https://victoriasreadingalcove.com/

Haunted by the heritage of a Romani grandmother, Adams seeks the healer, the herb maker, and the keeper of legends in whatever culture or faith tradition they may be found. Through the eyes of these practitioners, Adams explores the fuzzy-sharp edge between legend and life, between ritual and spirituality.

Adams lives and works on the Washington coast. Between visits to the beach and mountains of the Olympic Peninsula, she spends time with her fictional characters and a feline tuxedo named Sir Linus. She is a poet and a published author of two nonfiction titles, *Who I Am Yesterday: A Path to Coping With a Loved One's Dementia* and *Redefining Job and the Conundrum of Suffering*. She has published two short stories, *The Sketcher*, and *The Stargazer*. Her exploration of the world and ideas in general can be found at victoriasreadingalcove.com.

DAHLIA AGUILAR

Contact: dahliaaguilar71@gmail.com | @acocotli

Dahlia Aguilar hails from Corpus Christi. Dahlia's work is being published in *Naugatuck Review Winter/ Spring 2024*, *Somos Xicanas 2024* and *Boundless: the Anthology of the Rio Grande Valley International Poetry Festival*. She recently attended *Under the Volcano*, a writing residency in Tepoztlan, Mexico. She is a consultant and writer living in Deanwood, Washington DC with her son, two dogs, and menopause.

SHAVAWN M. BERRY

Contact: shavawnberry@gmail.com | https://thewonderlandfiles.com

Shavawn M. Berry writes poetry, prose, personal essays, & creative nonfiction. Her first collection of poetry, *Evanescent Creature*, was published by *Golden Dragonfly Press* in March of 2023. Her writing has previously appeared in Sable Books' anthology, *Red Sky – Poetry on the Global Epidemic of Violence Against Women*; *The Urban Howl*; *Trickster Literary Journal*; *The Huffington Post (HuffPo 50)*; *elephant journal*; *Rebelle Society*; *Olentangy Review*; *Journey of Heart: Women's Spiritual Poetry*; *Black Fox Literary Magazine*; *The Cancer Poetry Project 2*; *Poet Lore*; *Westview – A Journal of Western Oklahoma*; *North Atlantic Review*; and *Concho River Review*. She lives in Albuquerque, New Mexico.

LUPE CARRASCO CARDONA

Contact: lupeycardona@gmail.com | @lupe_teaches_ethnic_studies | www.guadalupecardona.com

Lupe Carrasco Cardona is an award-winning Ethnic Studies educator of 24 years who was presented the California Teachers Association Cesar Chavez, "SI SE PUEDE" Human Rights Award in 2022 and the National Education Association Foundation Award For Teaching Excellence Award in 2023. Lupe is the chair of the Association of Raza Educators (LA) and founding member of the Liberated Ethnic Studies Model Curriculum Coalition. She earned a BA in Chicanx and Latin American Studies from UCLA and a MA in Curriculum/Instruction, Language and Literacy from ASU. She is now pursuing a doctorate in Educational Leadership at CSUN. Lupe has spent her life and career remembering herself through storytelling and helps others on their quest to tell their own stories.

RAÚL CARDONA

Contact: raulscardona@gmail.com

Raúl Cardona is an artist and educator from Southern California. He has performed across the US including Denver Center for the Performing Arts, Round House Theatre, Seattle Repertory, Portland Center Stage, San Diego Rep, South Coast Rep, Center Theatre Group, Frida Kahlo Theatre, Company of Angels, Los Angeles Theatre Center and El Teatro Campesino.

VANCE COUPERUS

Contact: vancecouperus@gmail.com | https://twitter.com/VanceCouperus

Vance Couperus has works included in *Poetry*, *The Harvard Advocate*, and other publications. Vance graduated summa cum laude from UC Denver with a BA in Theater, Film, & Television and was awarded a Master's degree with distinction in Creative Writing from Durham University in the UK. Raised in the rural mountains of northern New Mexico.

Vance currently resides in Albuquerque.

MERIAH LYSISTRATA CRAWFORD

Contact: meriah@rhinoi.com | www.meriahcrawford.com

Meriah Lysistrata Crawford is a professor at Virginia Commonwealth University in the Department of Focused Inquiry, as well as a writer, editor, and private investigator. Among her publications are short stories in several genres, essays, poems, digital multimedia projects, a variety of scholarly work, and the co-written novel *The Persistence of Dreams*. Meriah has an MFA in creative writing from the University of Southern Maine's Stonecoast MFA program, and a PhD in literature and criticism from the Indiana University of Pennsylvania.

JOSHUA ALLEN DELEEUW

Contact: joshdeleeuw@icloud.com

Joshua Allen DeLeeuw is a writer and musician. He lives off grid in Taos New Mexico with his eight-year-old daughter. His writing is focused on trauma and the power of creativity to heal and transform trauma into art. Tell your story and be the change.

SHARON ELLIOTT

Contact: sharonseewater@gmail.com

Sharon Elliott is a Seattle author and international poet who now resides in Albuquerque, New Mexico. She has been a writer and poet activist over several decades beginning in the anti-war and civil rights movements in the 1960s and 70s. She spent four years in the Peace Corps in Nicaragua and Ecuador, and her writing focuses on multicultural women's issues. She was a Moderator of Poets Responding to SB1070, and has featured in poetry readings in the San Francisco Bay area, Los Angeles, Seattle, Redmond, Albuquerque, Cuba and Scotland. Her work has been published in several anthologies and her poem *Border Crossing* appears in the anthology entitled *Poetry of Resistance: Voices for Social Justice*, Francisco X. Alarcón and Odilia Galván Rodriguez, eds. She has read it in Los Angeles at AWP and the La Pachanga 2016 book launch, in San Francisco, at the Féis Seattle (Scots gaelic language/culture workshop) Céiliedh in Port Townsend, WA and at Poetry Express in Berkeley.

Her poetry has been published in many print journals domestically and internationally (in Cuba and Scotland) and has been translated into 4 languages. Her chapbook, *Jaguar Unfinished*, was published in 2012 by Prickly Pear Publishing.

SUSAN HUTCHINSON

Contact: Susnhutchinson@aol.com | 189 Center Rd., Shirley, MA 01464

There are those who claim that Susan A. Hutchinson is an unconventional poet, writer and verifiable sage, perennially seeking the whereabouts of truth and justice. Others say she simply likes pen and ink, fish and frogs. Susan lives in Shirley, MA and will be publishing her first novel about Minkey, a chimpanzee on a world mission, in the near future.

VERONICA EVANS AKA KALIFA KANDAKAT-JI

Contact: KalifaKandakat@gmail.com | Chitowndesertgirl2003@gmail.com

Kalifa is a creative, humanist, life coach, philosopher, public speaker, successor, and writer focusing on assisting others in their mutual quest to understand and master the complexities of faith in American society. She served as a writer for an international peace organization for 14 years, and later as its Midwest Bureau Chief for an additional 17 years, while based in her adopted hometown of Chicago, Illinois. Kalifa is currently a Member Care Advisor and a 54 year Nichiren Buddhist supporting other peace workers in Southern California.

She presented her poem, *Humor in Death,* on the stage of Claremont McKenna College for *KPCC In Person, Unheard LA*, a live storytelling series sponsored by *LAist*. Her lyrical poem, *Dear George*, dedicated to George Floyd on the anniversary of his death, was recently published in *These Black Bodies Are...A Blacklandia Anthology,* and was read at the *George Floyd Memorial* site in Minneapolis in 2023.

Ever the multitasker, Kalifa is seeking a publisher for her first book of poetry entitled *Peacock Writings: The Fragile Heart of a Poet, An Anthology*, in addition to her first set of ekphrastic poems entitled *The Ecstasy of Ekphrastic*. In her spare time, she is writing a nonfiction due for completion in the fall of 2024.

KENNADY KNIGHT

Contact: kennadyrknight@gmail.com

Kennady Knight is a sixteen-year-old high school student and one of New Mexico's rising young poets. She has attended three years of Baca Retreats and is honing her craft toward a magnificent future.

She intends to go to Columbia College of UNM to achieve her career in Creative Writing and screenplay while also hoping to have her own book of poetry published. She has a writing TikTok online (*Kenns writing*) that seems to reach the audience who relates to her writing. Looking toward a dynamic future, she understands that everything in her life has tremendous value and can be the source from which poetic license matures.

MELINA MARTINEZ

Contact: melinamartin@msn.com

Melina Martinez was raised in the arroyos, mountains and streams of the Sangre De Cristo Mountains and is of mixed descent with deep New Mexico lineages. A mother of two, wife and companion of over 32 years, Melina attended the University of Nevada Las Vegas where she earned her Doctor of Dental Medicine degree. She is a practicing dentist in Santa Fe New Mexico where she resides. Melina, a poet in grade school returned to her first love of writing upon returning to her native mountains. Melina has published her first book *Within My Shadows, Into my Light* and is working on her second.

J.D. MATHES

Contact: Jdmathes2@gmail.com | www.jdmathes.com

J.D. Mathes grew up a feral child in the deserts of the American Southwest who loved to read library books and take photographs. He is a PEN America Writing for Justice Fellow, an award-winning author of four books, photographer, screenwriter, and librettist. His memoir, *Ahead of the Flaming Front: A Life on Fire*, awarded the North American Book Prize for Memoir. Although Mathes still struggles with subject-verb agreement and where to put commas, he is currently working on a book, *Ill Served: Veterans and Mass Incarceration*, exploring justice involved veterans. He loves his two daughters very much.

MARIO MONTOYA

Contact: sol1@unm.edu | sol1921.wixsite.com/website

Mario Montoya is a teacher, writer and MC, and the 2021 recipient of the Rudolfo Anaya Fellowship, honoring promising New Mexican authors. He's a proud Burqueno (Albuquerque resident) where he received his MFA in Creative Writing from the University of New Mexico in July 2021. His work has appeared in numerous books, anthologies, journals and websites. In 2021, his poem *Prayer for the Guilty* was published by *Free Them All Poetry Series,* next to a Spanish translation.

When he's not teaching or writing, he's doing Hip Hop or making tortillas. Or watching the Raiders lose while playing sad jazz on his record player, when he should be grading.

BRIANA MUÑOZ

Contact: brianamunozwriting@gmail.com | https://linktr.ee/Awomanofwords

Briana Muñoz is a poet from Southern California and author of two books of poetry including *Loose Lips* (Prickly Pear Publishing) and *Everything is Returned to the Soil* (FlowerSong Press).

Briana is the founder of Poetry as Harm Reduction and currently serving as the Board of Directors Secretary for the Los Angeles Poet Society.

DR. NADINE PHOENIX

Contact: nadinephoenix22@gmail.com

Dr. Nadine Phoenix stands at the crossroads of science and creativity, distinguishing herself as both a Biology Teaching Assistant Professor at Portland State University, and as an inspired creative writer and artist. Her multifaceted career also includes a significant role as a career mentor, Faculty Senator, and involvement in numerous university committees.

Her academic journey was notably enriched by a postdoctoral fellowship at Stanford University School of Medicine, where she pioneered in studying placental physiology through maternal exosomes and earning academic grants and awards throughout her career.

Earning her Ph.D. in Molecular, Cellular, and Developmental Biology from the University of California, Santa Barbara, Dr. Phoenix specialized in underwater adhesion using Chemical Engineering principles. As a first-generation college graduate, she deeply empathizes with the challenges encountered by students, dedicating herself to nurturing their scientific and personal growth.

Beyond her scientific and mentoring achievements, Dr. Phoenix's engagement in writing and art not only showcases her diverse talents but also enriches her teaching and mentoring approach, offering a holistic educational experience. Her ability to weave together the rigor of science with the nuances of creative expression makes her an invaluable asset to her students and peers, embodying the spirit of a modern Renaissance woman.

CHRISTIANNA ORTIZ

Contact: Ntrs.hd757@gmail.com

Ms. Otiz has a Master's Degree in Special Education with a concentration in learning/ behavioral exceptionalities. She has a true passion for supporting and collaborating with students, administration, educators, staff, cadre, and parents towards implementation of appropriate strategies to meet the needs of students.

She takes pride in compassionate responsiveness regarding the diverse strengths of all learners. The ChalleNGe team is integral in empowering Cadets to realize their dreams.

Mama to two exquisite human beings, family tamalada promoter, undercover supershero, obsessed with all things TACO, thrill seeker, memory maker, Paw-fectionist to two Chinese Crested's (Bartok the Magnificent and Woodstock), and a spunky, mischievous black cat (Wednesday).

RONNIE ORTIZ

Contact: Ravens.N.RedChile@hotmail.com

Ronnie Ortiz Norteña de Nuevo Mexico has been called a wild child, a loose cannon, and real. Previously published in Hyperactive Music Magazine, prose and poetry in La Herencia del Norte, and food reviews in Examiner.com (New Mexico). Presented with Jimmy Santiago Baca, Tara Trudell, and Darryl Wellington at New Mexico Folk Art Museum in 2023. And she's only getting warmed up and diversified.

IVY RAFF

Contact: Ivy.raff@gmail.com | www.ivyraff.com/

Ivy Raff is the author of *What Remains / Qué queda* (bilingual English/Spanish edition, Editorial DALYA forthcoming 2024), winner of the Alberola International Poetry Prize, and *Rooted and Reduced to Dust* (Finishing Line Press, 2024). Individual poems appear in *ONE ART*, *The American Journal of Poetry*, Electric Literature's *The Commuter*, *Nimrod International Journal*, and West Trade Review, among numerous others, as well as in the anthologies *Spectrum: Poetry Celebrating Identity*, *Kinship: Poems on Belonging* (Renard Press, 2022 & 2023), *London Independent Story Prize Anthology* (LISP, 2023), and *Aesthetica*

Creative Writing Prize Annual (Aesthetica, 2023). As a Jewish artist and a human, Ivy advocates and agitates for a free Palestine. Mainly nomadic, she calls Queens, New York home.

MANNY REY

Contact: fashafilms@gmail.com | www.mannyrey.com

Manny Rey, poet-novelist-screenwriter-actor, resides in Encinitas, California. Manny's poetry collections, *In the Name of the Father, the Son, and Everything Raza* and *El Chuco: Chicano Poems That Are Chido* have been published by Honu Cove Press. *DREAD*, his latest work, is a horror novella that is hot off the press. Manny most recently completed filming on two movies in Panama, and look out for two upcoming works, *Out of Body Graffiti*--a poetry collection, as well as an upcoming novel, *IMMIGRANT BLOOD: A Story of Blood and Water.*

RONALDO ROYBAL

Contact: Roybal.ron@gmail.com

Ronaldo Roybal is a poet who grew up on a small farm in northern New Mexico. He is known for his accomplishments as an endurance athlete in track and cross country. He is a New Mexico high school state champion and All-American representing his hometown of Pojoaque. He competed for the University of Colorado where he earned NCAA All-American status and qualified for the Olympic Trials in the 5k. Today he lives and works in Boulder, Colorado where he is raising his son and writing poetry.

STACIE L. SANCHEZ

Contact: efd@staciesanchez.com

Stacie L. Sanchez is a lifelong New Mexico resident, who has enjoyed brief interludes of living in a few other states over the years, including Little Rock Arkansas. She holds a Bachelor of Art with a major in Studio Art and a minor in Creative Writing. She has focused much of her adult life building a visual art career as a working artist and educator.

She is currently teaching 4th grade for a New Mexico public school in a remote location where she enjoys the diverse culture of her native students, the mountain air and talking to the deer as they graze in her front yard. She is preparing to open her studio/gallery and small art school in her hometown of Grants, New Mexico.

Stacie will also be starting her graduate program in May pursuing her MFA in creative writing along with a certificate concentration of teaching for university online programs.

DARRYL LORENZO WELLINGTON

Contact: darrylwellington@hotmail.com

Darryl Lorenzo Wellington was the 6th Poet Laureate of Santa Fe, NM. His chapbook, *Life's Prisoners,* received the 2017 Turtle Island Quarterly award. His full-length poetry collections are *Psalms at the Present Time* (2021) and *Legible Walls* (2023).

FLOWERSONG
P R E S S

**FlowerSong Press nurtures essential verse
from, about, and throughout the borderlands.
Literary. Lyrical. Boundless.**

Sign up for announcements about
new and upcoming titles at:

www.flowersongpress.com

www.ingramcontent.com/pod-product-compliance
Lightning Source LLC
Chambersburg PA
CBHW081336120626
46546CB00011B/3367